THREE ACROSS

THREE
ACROSS

The Great

Transatlantic

Air Race

of 1927

Norman H. Finkelstein

CALKINS CREEK
Honesdale, Pennsylvania

For Risa and Ken

ACKNOWLEDGMENTS

I wish to acknowledge the following for their invaluable assistance:

Dr. Jeremy R. Kinney, curator of the Aeronautics Division,
National Air and Space Museum, Smithsonian Institution, Washington, D.C.,
for his careful review of this book.

William Wagner of the Ryan Aeronautical Library, a division of
Teledyne Ryan, San Diego, California.

The Minnesota Historical Society, St. Paul, Minnesota.

The staff of the National Air and Space Museum, Washington, D.C.

Carolyn Yoder, who edited this book with insight and skill.

My wife, Rosalind, for her continued understanding, patience, and
unwavering editorial eye.

Library of Congress Cataloging-in-Publication Data

Finkelstein, Norman H.
Three across : the great transatlantic air race of 1927 / By Norman H. Finkelstein.
p. cm.
Includes bibliographical references and index.
ISBN 978-1-59078-462-4 (hardcover : alk. paper)
1. Aeronautics—United States—History—Juvenile literature.
2. Transatlantic flights—Juvenile literature. I. Title.
TL521.F35 2008
629.130973—dc22
2007018345

CALKINS CREEK
An Imprint of Boyds Mills Press, Inc.
815 Church Street
Honesdale, Pennsylvania 18431

CONTENTS

CHAPTER 1   The Shortest Distance   7

CHAPTER 2   Next Stop, Europe   20

CHAPTER 3   Lucky Lindy   37

CHAPTER 4   "Well, Here We Are."   52

CHAPTER 5   "To Berlin! To Berlin!"   66

CHAPTER 6   "Far Enough!"   74

CHAPTER 7   Close Enough   88

CHAPTER 8   Glory!   101

CHAPTER 9   Frontier of Flight   114

Author's Note   123

Source Notes   124

Bibliography   128

Index   130

Text Credits   133

Picture Credits   134

1

THE SHORTEST DISTANCE

"I am attempting the flight to bring honor to French aviation."
—Charles Nungesser

Otto Lilienthal died in 1896 when his human-powered glider fell to the ground–killed in an air crash at a time when the modern airplane had not yet been invented. The idea of flight fascinated the German scientist since childhood. He carefully watched birds—their wing structures and movements—to understand some of the principles that could allow humans to fly. Lilienthal built and perfected airborne gliders based on his observations of the lifting power of a bird's wings. His writings on aeronautics were avidly read by flight enthusiasts around the world. Wilbur Wright later said, "My own active interest in aeronautical problems dates back to the death of Lilienthal in 1896."

Orville and Wilbur Wright refined Lilienthal's work and added a simple motor to their glider. In 1903, at Kitty Hawk, North Carolina, Orville flew unsteadily a few feet over the ground and inaugurated the aviation age. "This flight," Orville Wright said, "lasted only 12 seconds, but it was nevertheless the first in the history of the world in which a machine carrying a man had raised itself by its own power into the air in full flight, and sailed forward without reduction of speed, and had finally landed at a point as high as that from which it started."

Human flight had been a dream since the dawn of time. In Greek mythology, the story of Daedalus and Icarus, the father and son who attempt to escape imprisonment by flying away on wings of wax and feathers, is a reminder of that dream's power. Young Icarus, ignoring the obvious danger, became an early air casualty when his wings melted as he flew too close to the sun. For centuries thereafter, attempts at human flight usually met with similar disaster. But that did not prevent people from dreaming of the day when they might, like birds, be able to fly.

During the Renaissance period in Europe, the famed artist, thinker, and inventor Leonardo da Vinci (1452–1519) created detailed drawings of imaginative inventions that would allow humans to imitate birds in flight. In the eighteenth century, balloonists began experimenting with heated-air flights that for the first time allowed humans to soar above the ground for extended periods—but not without disasters. Although people could now go aloft, they found that heading for a specific destination was a problem, since they could not easily steer the balloon and relied mainly on prevailing and ever-changing air currents for direction.

In quick succession, after the Wright brothers' historic flight in 1903, aviation enthusiasts began building bigger planes with bigger engines. Their goal was to fly even farther and higher. Each new record advanced the growth of aviation. In 1909, the French aviator Louis Blériot (1872–1936) flew his homemade plane across the English Channel from Calais, France, to Dover, England. It took him thirty-seven minutes to fly the twenty-five miles. More importantly, his flight demonstrated how aviation could join two countries, even when separated by an impressive body of water. As aviation grew, so did the size of the body of water that began to challenge pilots.

Public enthusiasm for flight also grew. In 1913, the *London Daily Mail* offered a $50,000 prize to the first person to cross the Atlantic Ocean by airplane, in either direction, between any point in the United States, Canada, or the Canadian province of Newfoundland and any point in Great Britain or Ireland. The only rule was that the flight had to be made in seventy-two continuous hours or less. Any thought of attempting this record-setting flight had to be put aside with the outbreak of the Great War (World War I) in 1914.

While record-breaking flights had to wait, the war provided its own impetus to the growth of aviation. Before the war, there were only a handful of airplanes in the United States. During the war, each of the major participants, Great

Britain, France, the United States, and Germany, feverishly trained thousands of new pilots and built increasingly more sophisticated and reliable airplanes. Aviation technology revolutionized warfare forever.

René-Paul Fonck

The most honored French aviator of World War I was first to announce a try for the Orteig Prize.

Each country had its own set of aviation war heroes whose bravery in the air impressed both soldiers and civilians. In Germany, the fearless flying of the "Red Baron," Baron Manfred von Richthofen, and the ingenious airplanes designed by Dutch designer Anthony Fokker raised hopes of victory. All of France was captivated by the daring adventures of aviators René-Paul Fonck and Charles Nungesser. Once the United States entered the war in 1917, the exploits of air ace Captain Edward V. Rickenbacker filled the newspapers. His selfless leadership was legendary. "I should never ask any pilot under me to go on a mission that I myself would not undertake," he later said.

When the war ended in 1918, thousands of military aviators found themselves out of work and out of aviation. Public interest in aviation continued, but with the war won, the United States government scaled down dramatically much of the aviation design and research begun during the war, largely to save money. But it could not end the interest in flying. Fliers, with few opportunities to practice their skills, bought up surplus military aircraft from the government for as little as fifty dollars apiece. For the next few years, daring fliers barnstormed the surplus planes around the country, offering rides and performing in air shows and circuses. Pilots such as Clarence Chamberlin and Charles A. Lindbergh honed their aviation skills as they traveled from one flying job to another.

In 1919, in an attempt to bolster the image of aviation and increase funding from the U.S. Congress, U.S. Navy pilots made plans to fly over the Atlantic. With military precision and detail, Seaplane Division Number 1 prepared for the hazardous trip. Three identical two-wing hydroplanes, built by the Curtiss Company and designed to land and take off from water, were to fly together for safety. They would not attempt a nonstop flight, but would make three stops on their way across. The planes, designated NC-1, NC-3, and NC-4 (*NC* an abbreviation for *Navy Curtiss*), were scheduled to take off from Trepassey Bay in Newfoundland for the Azores (islands off the coast of Portugal); then from the Azores to Lisbon, Portugal; and finally from Lisbon to Plymouth, England. (The NC-2 proved not to be airworthy and was used for spare parts.) All along the route, over sixty naval destroyers were deployed at fifty-mile intervals to act as navigational beacons and provide help if needed. From the moment the planes took off from Trepassey Bay on May 16, 1919, the pilots faced two problems: forecasting the weather in their flight path and unexpected mechanical problems. The NC-1 and NC-3 each made crash landings into the sea. Only the NC-4 reached Plymouth. It took 52 hours and 31 minutes of actual flight time, but the plane eventually landed safely on May 31. The crew received great ovations in Europe, but skepticism back home. While offering his congratulations, President Woodrow Wilson also gave them, and all aviators, the cautious advice "not to get too high, for the higher you get the harder the fall will be."

Thanks to its unique geographic distinction—the easternmost part of North America and therefore the closest across the Atlantic to Europe—Newfoundland became the center of world aviation during May of 1919. However, Newfoundland's picturesque rocky hills also offered significant drawbacks. One British pilot later recalled, "Newfoundland is a hospitable place but its best friends cannot claim that it is ideal for aviation." Aside from the NC flights, four English teams in Newfoundland made ready for the transatlantic hop that could earn one of them the *London Daily Mail* prize for the first nonstop flight across the Atlantic. Because of mechanical problems, only two managed to take off.

One plane, a Sopwith biplane, the *Atlantic*, took off on May 18, 1919, from St. John's, Newfoundland. Aboard were two capable fliers, Harry Hawker and Kenneth Mackenzie-Grieve. Once aloft, they, too, experienced constant weather problems and soon disappeared from sight. The plane and its brave pilots were presumed downed somewhere in the vast, cold Atlantic. Eventually, to everyone's surprise and delight, Hawker and Mackenzie-Grieve arrived safely in England—by boat. They had been forced down into the water but were rescued by a Danish freighter, which had no radio. Not until the ship approached England on May 26 did the world learn that the fliers were safe. The *Daily Mail* prize was yet to be won.

On June 14, 1919, Captain John Alcock and Lieutenant Arthur Whitten Brown of the British Royal Air Force took off from St. John's, Newfoundland, in a Vickers-Vimy biplane, which had two sets of wings—one upper and one lower—separated by struts and wires to provide increased structural integrity. Their goal: Ireland, a shorter destination than England but one which would certainly qualify as a transatlantic flight. It was not an easy trip. Shortly after takeoff, a small but important propeller that powered the plane's simple radio fell into the ocean. The radio's range was limited anyway, so once over the Atlantic it really didn't matter. For the rest of their harrowing journey the plane flew in fog and clouds so thick, it was nearly impossible for them to know where they were.

A piece of exhaust pipe then blew away, allowing flames to dance around the plane's canvas outer covering. The plane could disintegrate in flames at any moment. On they flew. Farther along, after pulling the plane from a near crash landing into the water, they discovered ice forming on the wings and blocking vents and instrument gauges. Several times, Brown had to climb out of the cockpit in midflight, hang on to a strut, and knock the ice away. Nearly sixteen hours after leaving Newfoundland, Alcock tapped his partner and pointed into the distance. "I followed the direction indicated by his outstretched forefinger;" Brown recalled, "and barely visible through the mist, it showed me two tiny specks of—land."

Even their landing was far from perfect. From the air they sighted an open area on the ground that appeared to provide a perfect spot. Only when the tires touched ground did they discover that they had landed in a soft, mucky bog. The plane tipped over and its nose burrowed into the soppy ground. Nonetheless, Alcock and Brown had done it—crossed the Atlantic Ocean, 1,680 miles, nonstop—in 15 hours, 57 minutes. "We have had a terrible journey," Alcock said. "The wonder is we are here at all." They returned to London as national heroes. At Windsor Castle, King George V knighted them, and Winston Churchill, secretary of state for war and air, presented them with a check for the *Daily Mail* prize.

Today, as jumbo jets effortlessly make their way to remote airfields, it is easy to forget how unprepared the world was in the 1920s for aviation. Early airplanes were quite fragile and built as biplanes, an aircraft with two sets of wings to provide increased stability. They were constructed of light materials and were incapable of supporting much weight. They did not have a fuselage, or hollow tube body to hold all the pieces of the craft together and carry people and cargo. Airplane designers began experimenting with aerodynamic shapes. Ongoing advances were made in engine and fuselage technology. As the designs evolved, plane fuselages became longer and stronger. Experiments with single-wing, or monoplane, aircraft reduced air resistance, or drag, while in flight. There still were no air-route maps, radar, guidance systems, and airport networks. Night flying was virtually unknown, limited to harebrained daredevil fliers. Most Americans couldn't conceive of the airplane as a viable form of passenger trans-portation. Nor could they imagine a time when thousands of airplanes would crisscross the country daily.

The closest the United States could come to a cross-country airline system was the one established by the U.S. Post Office Department's airmail service. In the early 1920s, the department's civilian pilots—many were trained by the military during World War I—performed daring flying feats to deliver the mail. They flew over dangerous mountain ranges, through the most inclement weather, and landed in meadows hastily converted to makeshift airfields. Some died delivering the mail; others were involved in spectacular accidents. Despite these setbacks, slowly but steadily the United States became linked by a growing network of air routes.

The chief pilot of the Robertson Aircraft Corporation, the post office contractor on the St. Louis–Chicago link in 1925, was a twenty-three-year-old young man by the name of Charles A. Lindbergh. Lindbergh was born on February 4,

Young Charles Lindbergh and his mother

Evangeline Lindbergh was a constant source of support for her son. She later became a schoolteacher in Detroit.

Two Lindberghs in Congress

Lindy's father, C. A. Lindbergh, was elected to the United States Congress in 1906. Here, young Charles (center top) is shown standing next to his father at the opening of the Sixtieth Congress in Washington, D.C.

1902, in Detroit, Michigan, and grew up in Little Falls, Minnesota, by the banks of the Mississippi River. He was tall and lanky and his friends called him Slim. Slim, who began piloting planes at the age of twenty, left college to pursue a flying career. He barnstormed around the Midwest in an army surplus plane he bought by trading in his motorcycle. He even performed in a flying circus. Wanting more formal training, he enlisted in the Army Air Service, formed in 1918, and graduated from flight school at the top of his class with a commission as a second lieutenant in the army reserve.

He flew lonely and danger-filled hops in and out of cow pastures and small makeshift airfields in all kinds of weather. On several occasions he had to parachute to safety when he ran out of fuel, sending his plane crashing to the ground.

After a crash

Like many barnstorming pilots, Charles Lindbergh experienced his share of crashes and accidents. Here he is standing beside his crashed airmail plane after an accident in 1925 (third from left). The young aviator safely parachuted to the ground just before the plane crashed into a field.

As he flew the lonely mail route, he began to think about the future of aviation and the recent attempts to demonstrate the efficacy of long-distance flying.

In 1924, not willing to be outdone by the navy, the U.S. Army Air Service began an ambitious endeavor: a carefully charted flight in small hops around the world. This flight would not only continue to focus world attention on aviation but also secure a place for army aviation in its competition with the navy. Four biplanes, specially built by the Douglas Aircraft Company, each with a crew of two and each named after a major American city (Boston, New Orleans, Seattle, and Chicago), took off from Seattle on April 6, 1924. Timing was essential. Weather and climate were carefully considered, and an east-to-west route was selected to allow the planes to cross Alaska and the Pacific Ocean before the onset of bad travel conditions.

An advance team provided emergency supplies and spare parts all along the route. Naval ships were constantly advised of the planes' positions in case rescue at sea was needed. But as with other flights of the era, weather and geography offered the greatest obstacles. Most of the flying time would be spent over uncharted terrain. The *Seattle* dropped out first after a crash landing on a snowy mountain slope in the Alaskan wilderness.

The three remaining planes made their way in short hops across the Aleutian Islands and into Siberia and on to Japan. They then crossed the Yellow Sea and stopped at Shanghai and Hong Kong. At each stop, the planes were met by enthusiastic crowds, and reports of their welcomes appeared in newspapers back in the United States. En route to Saigon, French Indochina, disaster struck again and the *Chicago* was temporarily out of the flight, awaiting an engine replacement. The other two planes continued on and were rejoined in Saigon a few days later by the repaired *Chicago*.

Throughout the summer and early fall of 1924, the three planes carried on their historic journey. Through the Middle East, into Europe, across the North Atlantic to Iceland, the intrepid fliers faced deserts, winds, fog, and icebergs. Off the coast of the Faroe Islands in the North Atlantic between Norway and Iceland, ships sailed to the rescue when the *Boston* had to make an emergency water landing. The crew made it safely onboard a naval vessel, but the airplane sank to the ocean bottom when attempts were made to hoist it aboard.

And then, there were two. The *New Orleans* and the *Chicago* headed to Greenland and then across North America toward their takeoff city, Seattle, Washington. In Nova Scotia, the two planes were joined by a replacement, called the *Boston II*. It was piloted by the two fliers of the original ill-fated *Boston*. In Washington, D.C., en route to Seattle, the crews and their planes were greeted by President Calvin Coolidge as they began the last legs of their transcontinental journey. They finally returned to Seattle on September 28, 1924, having flown 26,345 miles in 363 hours and 7 minutes. They had flown around the world and demonstrated that, with adequate preparation and better equipment, long-distance flight was not an idle dream. Their accomplishments made it possible for younger pilots, like Lindbergh, as well as other citizens to imagine the future.

In 1926, Slim Lindbergh began to consider the possibility of a flight to Paris and winning the Orteig Prize. In 1919, shortly after World War I, a wealthy French-born New York hotel owner, Raymond Orteig, offered $25,000 to the first person to fly nonstop between New York and Paris. The prize was valid for five years, but since it was unclaimed by the end of 1924, Orteig renewed his offer for yet another five years.

During his lonely mail trips over the Midwest, Lindbergh began forming the scenario for just such a daring flight. For him, advances in airplane design and the availability of more reliable and efficient engines made this the right time. A flight to Paris could succeed, he reasoned, because of "the modern radial air-cooled motor, high lift airfoils and lightened construction, it would not only be possible to reach Paris but, under normal conditions, to land with a large reserve of fuel and have a high factor of safety throughout the entire trip as well."

The Wright Aeronautical Corporation, founded by the Wright brothers, was the builder of the nearly foolproof Whirlwind air-cooled radial engine. Its simplicity, reliability, light weight—no radiator system, cooling fluid, or water pump needed—and efficient use of fuel made it ideal for long-distance flight. The engine's cylinders were arranged around the propeller shaft like the spokes of a wheel. In flight, the exposed cylinders were cooled by onrushing air, which carried away heat. In early May 1926, Arctic explorer Commander Richard E. Byrd, with famed pilot Floyd Bennett at the controls, flew a Fokker single-wing plane powered by three Wright J-4 Whirlwind engines for 15 hours and 30 minutes over ice-strewn wasteland heading for the North Pole. Byrd later said that his choice of engines "added to our chances of success." A year later, an improved version of the Whirlwind J-4, the J-5, would power most of the planes attempting to cross the Atlantic.

Reports of the Byrd flight captured the interest and imagination of newspaper readers back home. When the two fliers arrived back in the United States in June, they were national heroes. President Coolidge presented them with distinguished medals on behalf of the National Geographic Society, founded in 1888 and dedicated to the support of scientific exploration. In New York, they marched down Broadway in a ticker-tape parade while thousands cheered. Truly, long-distance flight was of public interest.

By 1926, owing primarily to the advances made in airplane technology, first entry forms for the Orteig Prize began to arrive at the New York headquarters of the Aero Club, charged with administering the race. On both sides of the Atlantic, eager teams of aviators began to make plans and arrange financial support for their individual projects. But a series of disastrous accidents and deaths kept postponing the award of the Orteig Prize.

On September 21, 1926, French war ace René-Paul Fonck sat at the controls of a big Sikorsky S-35 multiengine plane as it rolled down Roosevelt Field on Long Island, New York, for a test flight. Onboard the sixteen-passenger plane were three other crewmen, Charles Clavier, Lawrence Curtin, and Jacob Islamoff. The plane had never been aloft with such a heavy load of supplies and fuel, but other competing planes were being readied. Igor Sikorsky, the Russian-born airplane designer, preferred more months of intensive testing for his plane, but pressure on him to win the Orteig Prize was too great and time was running out.

The huge, heavily loaded plane lumbered awkwardly down the runway. By the time it reached the end of Roosevelt Field, it still had not gathered enough speed to lift off the ground. Without brakes (planes then didn't have any), the choices for Fonck were limited. He could turn the plane and abort the takeoff or risk the dangers and continue forward. But so many people had crowded onto all parts of the field to watch the takeoff that Fonck couldn't risk turning. So he kept gathering speed and rolled toward the adjoining Curtiss Field. The problem Fonck had not anticipated was that the two fields were separated by a twenty-foot drop. The plane disappeared from sight into the gully as onlookers, including Sikorsky, held their breaths from afar. Suddenly, flames and smoke shot into the sky as the spectators rushed forward. When the smoke cleared, the plane was destroyed, and two of the four crewmen, Clavier and Islamoff, were dead. Fonck barely escaped with his life.

Despite the horrible accident, aviators focused on their goal, and 1926 ended with the expectation that the new year would see the Orteig Prize finally won.

Lindbergh and Fonck

Lindbergh is shown with René-Paul Fonck, the pilot of the ill-fated Sikorsky plane that crashed upon takeoff at Roosevelt Field, killing two of the four crew members.

2

NEXT STOP, EUROPE

"This is the moment I've planned for."
—Charles A. Lindbergh

To most Long Islanders today, Roosevelt Field is a huge shopping center. Acres of parking surround the department stores in the mall, which draws thousands of visitors each day. As shoppers come and go, few realize that decades earlier Roosevelt Field was the center of a different kind of activity.

Land in that part of Long Island is flat and largely treeless, ideal for airplane takeoffs and landings. As aviation developed just prior to World War I, chunks of the then undeveloped land were sectioned off as airfields. Over the years, these fields underwent name changes and merged into larger fields to accommodate the growth of aviation. The original Hempstead Plains Aerodrome became Hazelhurst Field, and in 1921 the western part of it was renamed Curtiss Field after the aircraft manufacturer that purchased it. The adjoining field to the east was named Roosevelt Field in 1918 to honor former president Theodore Roosevelt's son, a pilot killed during World War I. To the south was Mitchel Field, a military airfield established in 1917.

New hangars began to encircle the fields during the early 1920s, signs of increased interest and technological advances in aviation. The flying techniques learned during World War I, coupled with changes in engine and airplane designs, brought aviation to a new level of activity. As airplane engines became more powerful and reliable, aviators began thinking of larger implications. The dream of flying longer distances with heavier loads, perhaps even scheduled passenger services to rival the railroads, was about to be realized.

But before aviation could progress, people had to be convinced there was a serious future for airplanes beyond the barnstormer and air circus stage.

Flying over the Atlantic would obviously boost aviation's prestige. But first, an airplane had to be built with the power and strength to carry at least twice its weight in fuel to successfully fly across the ocean. By the mid-1920s, daring pilots on both sides of the Atlantic were ready for the challenge of flying across first. There had been several successful shorter Atlantic flights, but also a number of dramatic failures and deaths. With new technical advances in airplane design and engine performance, aviators in the United States and Europe prepared to reap glory.

Because of their location, Roosevelt and Curtiss fields were natural takeoff sites for flights from the United States to Europe. By mid-March 1927, competing technical teams began to set up operations at the fields. These were newsworthy events, and reporters covered every angle of every anticipated flight. On April 10, the *New York Times* reported extensively on flights scheduled to take off from Roosevelt Field, although the planes had not yet arrived. The best-known team was headed by Commander Richard E. Byrd. Byrd and his crew were in New Jersey preparing to run tests on their multiengined plane, the *America*. Commander Byrd was the most cautious of the potential contenders. He saw the flight of the *America* as a scientific undertaking that would demonstrate that long-distance passenger aviation was not only feasible but safe. He purposely selected a large, multiengined plane and made plans to outfit it with the latest navigational and radio equipment. With safety a key concern, he attended to the minutest detail down to the medical supplies and rations for the flight. Accompanying him would be an experienced crew of three.

A second plane, a Keystone two-winged craft called the *American Legion* and piloted by Lieutenant Commander Noel Davis and Lieutenant Stanton H. Wooster, was undergoing similar tests in Pennsylvania.

Tucked away in the same edition of the newspaper was a brief announcement that on the West Coast a little-known pilot named Charles A. Lindbergh was beginning flight tests on a plane called the *Spirit of St. Louis*. It was designed and built by the equally little-known Ryan Airlines to compete for the Orteig Prize.

Ryan Airlines

The small San Diego, California, company rose to the challenge to build the *Spirit of St. Louis* in this old, makeshift factory.

Yet another plane, known as the Wright-Bellanca, was about to enter the race. It was designed by Giuseppe Bellanca and owned by Charles A. Levine and his Columbia Aircraft Corporation. Levine was born in 1897 in North Adams, Massachusetts, but grew up in Brooklyn, New York. He was a self-made millionaire who made his fortune in the scrap-metal business at the end of World War I.

The plane, known also as the WB-2, was originally built by Bellanca for the Wright Aeronautical Corporation to specifically accommodate Wright's new ultradependable Whirlwind J-5 aircraft engine. When Wright decided to exit the plane-building business and concentrate solely on engines, Levine bought the plane and hired Bellanca. Levine's goal was to obtain a profitable United States airmail contract and then build more Bellancas for use on the route and to sell to other companies.

Because of its unique design, the Bellanca was considered a favorite to succeed across the ocean. Giuseppe Bellanca said, "My ideas of airplane design have been so radically different from conventional design that from the first I have been forced to prove their worth." The plane was constructed with a

Giuseppe Bellanca in the cockpit

The designer is shown in the cockpit of his Wright-Bellanca plane the *Columbia*.

steel-tube fuselage rather than the usual wood. Its powerful 220 horsepower Whirlwind engine was the best available. Indeed, before turning to Ryan Airlines in San Diego, Lindbergh had tried to buy the Wright-Bellanca from Levine. The attempt failed because Levine did not want his plane flown across the Atlantic by a crew of one. Lindbergh then turned to the unknown Ryan Airlines in California.

Interestingly, each American plane then preparing to fly across the Atlantic was powered by that same new revolutionary air-cooled engine. But aside from that similarity and obvious desire to cross the Atlantic first, each project was different. In the end, sheer luck, more than technical superiority, determined ultimate success. Each plane had its own tale of agonizing setbacks and problems.

While the *America* was being prepared and the *Spirit of St. Louis* was under construction, Charles A. Levine had a thought. If his Bellanca plane, so much sought after by Lindbergh, made it across the Atlantic first, the commercial success of the Columbia Aircraft Corporation would be assured. Clarence Chamberlin, the Bellanca pilot, later said that Levine "thought it would be a good idea to make a name for the ship before they put it into production." Levine, aware of public relations opportunities, began to design a scenario worthy of Hollywood.

First came the question of who would fly the plane. Levine, who had denied Lindbergh the opportunity to fly the Wright-Bellanca alone, wanted a crew of two for the long and lonely journey. Each aviator would have to be well known and photogenic for the film offers that would naturally follow the epic flight. His first choice was Leigh Wade, a renowned pilot who had been one of the crew of the multiplane 1924 flight around the world. A series of disagreements between Levine and Wade led to the pilot's hasty departure.

Towing the *Spirit*

The *Spirit of St. Louis* fuselage is towed to Dutch Flats Airfield by an automobile for the installation of the plane's wing.

His successor for one of the two pilot positions was Bert Acosta, another experienced flier. Levine and his new pilot immediately began arguing about nearly every flight detail. Before proceeding with the actual plans for a transatlantic flight, Levine needed to know whether the plane was as good as everyone thought, since the plane had never undergone a full-load distance test.

On April 12, 1927, the Bellanca plane took off from Roosevelt Field. Onboard were Clarence Chamberlin, another experienced pilot who had come over to Columbia Aircraft with Giuseppe Bellanca, and Bert Acosta from the Wright Aeronautical Corporation. The flight would determine if the plane could actually stay in the air long enough for a New York–Paris trip. It also needed to prove that the plane could actually take off with the heavy load of fuel necessary for such a long period aloft.

Putting the wing on the *Spirit of St. Louis*

The wing was installed at the Ryan Flying Company's hangar at the Dutch Flats Airfield, near San Diego, California. Ryan Flying Company was later known as Ryan Airlines.

When the plane safely returned to Roosevelt Field on April 14, after circling the area for 51 hours and 11 minutes, it had shattered the world's endurance record. It also attracted a lot of attention. Thousands of people greeted the fliers and swarmed around their plane. Reporters and photographers recorded the moment, which was replayed with great fanfare in newspapers all over the country. Levine was now convinced. His plane was in the race.

On April 16, 1927, in Teterboro, New Jersey, the *America* took off on its first test flight. With Anthony Fokker, the plane's world-famous designer, in the pilot's seat, Byrd and other crew members crowded onboard. They were seemingly unconcerned about the effect their weight and load balance might have on the plane's handling. On landing, with the weight of the crew concentrated up front, the plane's tail rose uncontrollably, and the plane tipped over onto its nose. There was severe damage, and Floyd Bennett, a key crew member who had flown with Byrd to the North Pole a year earlier, was badly injured. Commander Byrd escaped with a broken wrist. Although Fokker and the mechanics began to direct the repairs almost immediately, any possibility of the *America* taking off within a short period of time disappeared along with Bennett's hope of flying to Europe. Taking Bennett's place was Bert Acosta, who left Levine's employ, no longer willing to put up with the Bellanca owner's constant arguments.

Despite the setback to Commander Byrd, the undaunted Levine proceeded with his plans. Acosta was replaced by another pilot, Lloyd Bertaud. The Bellanca was well positioned to be the first plane across the Atlantic. Newspapers guessed which of the several pilots under consideration would be named the second pilot aboard. Because Levine intended to have his plane take off as quickly as possible, he was not legally qualified for the Orteig Prize, which required a sixty-day advance notice of flight. However, the Brooklyn Chamber of Commerce, also appreciating the possible public relations bonanza, put up a $15,000 prize in honor of Levine's Brooklyn roots.

On Sunday, April 24, Charles A. Levine, his wife, his in-laws, Clarence Chamberlin, mechanics, reporters, and a crowd of interested bystanders gathered on Curtiss Field. As news photographers crouched around the plane, nine-year-old Eloyse, Levine's daughter, smashed a bottle of ginger ale across the propeller hub of the Bellanca and officially christened the Wright-Bellanca plane with its new name, the *Columbia*.

With that, Eloyse and Grace Jonas, daughter of the Brooklyn Chamber of Commerce president, asked Clarence Chamberlin to take them up for a ride. The girls' parents didn't object. John Carisi, chief mechanic of Columbia Aircraft, jumped in with them and off they flew for a short ride around the fields. As those in the plane enjoyed the beautiful views, people on the ground looked up in horror. Unbeknown to Chamberlin and his passengers, a pin had sheared loose, and the plane's left wheel hung useless beneath them. A landing could be fatal.

Two mechanics on the ground realized the danger. They grabbed a spare wheel and flew up in a second plane. They pointed to the wheel in their hands and then to the useless wheel beneath the *Columbia*. "I wonder why those darn fools are waving a tire at me?" Chamberlin thought. It took a few minutes to grasp their strange message. Chamberlin, an experienced pilot, keenly aware of his responsibility for the young passengers aboard, made ready to bring the plane down. All eyes on the ground were riveted on the circling plane. Mrs. Levine, a handkerchief held to her mouth, sobbed nervously as Giuseppe Bellanca stood beside her, following the plane's flight through a pair of binoculars.

Chamberlin circled over neighboring Roosevelt Field, where fewer people were on the ground, and began dropping out the weighted sandbags that balanced the rear of the plane. As an ambulance and crash wagon loaded with rescue equipment followed from field to field below them, Chamberlin headed toward the adjacent Mitchel Field where military guards could control the crowds of onlookers fast approaching in automobiles from Roosevelt Field.

At the height of the drama, a reporter asked Bellanca what would happen to his own plans if the plane crashed. "To hell with the plane," the designer answered. "If those two children are safe, I do not care what happens."

"I told the girls not to be frightened," Chamberlin later said. Then he brought the plane in for a spectacular landing on the one good wheel. The plane sustained only minor damage and no one onboard was hurt. The girls, in fact, had a wonderful time. Chamberlin even thought they were actually disappointed the landing was so calm. "Thank you for the ride, Mr. Chamberlin," they politely said.

The parents were grateful, too. There seemed no question now that Chamberlin would be the second pilot. Yet Levine had to keep alive the public's curiosity surrounding the identity of the second pilot who would help take *Columbia* to Paris. In the end he could not refuse to let Chamberlin go with Bertaud. With each passing day it became increasingly possible that one of several remaining competitors might take off before the *Columbia*. Just two days after Eloyse Levine's airborne adventure, the *American Legion*, being readied for the Paris trip, crashed during a tragic test flight in Virginia. The two pilots, Davis and Wooster, were killed in the fiery crash. The series of accidents cast a pall over the three remaining competitors, whose efforts were now concentrated at Curtiss and Roosevelt fields.

Meanwhile, Levine prepared contracts for Bertaud and Chamberlin that created more conflict. According to the legal documents, the *Columbia*'s owner would become exclusive "manager" of the pilots' business affairs following the flight. Levine anticipated that the pilots would become popular national heroes. Although Bertaud and Chamberlin were upset, they were more concerned about the fact that no provision was made for life insurance policies to protect their wives in the event of a fatal accident. "You can sign it or not, just as you please," Levine coldly told them, "but if you don't sign, you don't fly!" The pilots, more interested in flying to Paris than the fine print of a contract, signed. They just wanted to take off.

Over the following weeks, the *Columbia* underwent a number of test flights as a new engine was broken in and a highly sensitive earth inductor compass was calibrated. The new compass, invented in 1924 by the Pioneer Instrument Company, was more stable and reliable than earlier magnetic compasses. A debate raged between Bertaud and Levine over the inclusion of a radio on the flight. Levine thought it would be a good idea, but Bertaud understood that radios were heavy and cumbersome. They also had limited transmitting range and would be practically useless over the desolate Atlantic.

Another concern of all the transatlantic fliers was the weight of the fuel load. An engineer at Ryan Airlines referred to Lindbergh's plane as "a flying gas tank." A long runway was necessary to gather enough speed to successfully lift the fuel-heavy plane into the air. In a spirit of generosity, Commander Byrd, whose financial backers had made exclusive arrangements for the use of Roosevelt Field, offered the field and its longer runway to the *Columbia* and the *Spirit of St. Louis.*

Byrd's quest for a scientific approach also led him to an exclusive contract with the United States Weather Bureau. The greatest problem facing all the potential Atlantic aviators was the weather. While it might appear sunny and clear in New York, storms and clouds over a plane's entire route had to be considered. Thick clouds, thunderstorms, and heavy winds created terrible weather conditions over the Atlantic in those early weeks of May. Even if a plane were ready to fly, the weather would keep it grounded. The science of meteorology was in its infancy and there were no regular, reliable weather reports then. The weather in one location could not be predicted farther out than a day or so. Thanks to Byrd, each of the transatlantic flights from Roosevelt Field grew to rely on the expertise of one man, government meteorologist Dr. James H. Kimball. No one dared attempt a takeoff for Europe from New York without the permission of "Doc" Kimball.

While waiting for the weather to clear, there appeared only one significant threat to *Columbia*'s position as the plane favored to fly first across the Atlantic. In France, two pilots, Charles Nungesser and François Coli, were prepared to fly their French-built plane, *l'Oiseau Blanc*—the *White Bird*—from Paris to New York. Nungesser, a revered World War I hero, was a French national treasure.

Nungesser realized that with the limited power of available engines, the most important factor was overall takeoff weight. "Fuel comes first," he explained. "Everything must be sacrificed to that. Unless I can carry enough petrol, I can't succeed." Nungesser and Coli took their white-painted plane for tests with increasingly greater weight loads. All the while they carefully monitored the latest situation of their American rivals across the ocean. French hopes were

Coli and Nungesser

The French aviation heroes François Coli (left) and Charles Nungesser are shown in their plane the *White Bird*. Painted on the fuselage is Nungesser's personal insignia, depicting a skull and crossbones, coffin, and candlesticks inside a heart.

nearly dashed when they heard that Chamberlin planned to fly the *Columbia* on May 4. At the last moment, however, bad weather conditions prevented a takeoff, and Nungesser and Coli breathed a sigh of relief.

Early in the morning of May 8, with reports of better weather, a crowd of onlookers gathered at Le Bourget Airfield just outside Paris in response to news that the *White Bird* was finally ready for the big flight. "Let's go," Nungesser said, hugging Coli, and they both climbed aboard. At about 5:18 a.m. the heavily loaded plane took to the air, clearing the end of the runway with little space to spare. Excitement on both sides of the Atlantic was at fever pitch. The French were proud that their two countrymen would be first to cross the Atlantic. The *New York Times* headlined the takeoff: "NUNGESSER OFF ON PARIS–NEW

Awaiting news
Anxious Parisians gather in front of the offices of the newspaper *Le Matin* to await news of Nungesser and Coli.

YORK HOP AT 5:17 A.M. ... HOPE TO BE HERE TOMORROW ..."

Americans looked on in awe and not a little disappointment. It appeared that the two French pilots were about to win the race and the Orteig Prize. New York, with mixed emotions, prepared for a gala welcome. Ships, flying colorful banners and flags, steamed back and forth in New York Harbor, ready to welcome the *White Bird*. The next day, banner headlines in French newspapers announced the triumphal arrival of the *White Bird* in New York. Details of the fliers' words, the greetings of American dignitaries, and the joyous noise of welcoming horns and sirens were fully reported. Citizens danced in the streets of Paris. Nungesser's mother said, "Luck has always been with my son." At Curtiss Field, Giuseppe Bellanca graciously told reporters, "I am glad and proud they have succeeded. Of course, I would have liked to have had our plane to be the first, but they deserve to win and I'm glad they did."

By May 10, it was clear that Nungesser and Coli had failed. Search planes and ships headed out to look for the missing fliers and their plane. It was presumed that they came down in the Atlantic or in the thick wilderness of coastal Canada. No trace could be found. The plane and the pilots seemed to have disappeared off the face of the earth, never to be seen again. The disappointment in France was heart wrenching. In the United States, sadness at the apparent deaths of fellow airmen was tempered by the reality that the Orteig Prize was yet to be won.

From late April into early May, the crew of the *Columbia* puttered and tested, experimented and debated: radio or no radio; detachable or permanent wheels. Then, as bad weather continued to prevail, they patiently waited for Dr. Kimball's OK. A temporary break in the weather was due on Friday, May 13, but a superstitious Levine refused to allow the plane to take off on "unlucky" Friday the thirteenth. The long wait gave Bertaud time to think and grow increasingly bitter over the contract he had signed with Levine. The pilot hired an attorney and the debate over its contents escalated. Because of the bad luck of the French team, the *Columbia* had a renewed chance for success, but competition was quickly closing in.

The *America*

A closeup view of the *America* in front of the America Transoceanic Company hangar at Roosevelt Field.

On May 12, amid great press fanfare, the two remaining American contender planes arrived at Roosevelt and Curtiss fields to join the *Columbia*. Commander Byrd's plane arrived from its test site at the Fokker factory in New Jersey. Charles Lindbergh attracted national attention by flying his plane across the country from San Diego to St. Louis in 14 hours and 25 minutes, breaking the existing speed record.

Shortly after eight that morning, the *Spirit of St. Louis* took to the air for New York. Lindbergh didn't want anyone beating him to the takeoff for Paris. Before he had left San Diego, he had told T. Claude Ryan, the builder of the *Spirit of St. Louis*, "Let's put everything into range. I don't need a very stable plane. ... I don't plan on going to sleep." With his arrival, the *New York Times* optimistically reported, "Three transatlantic planes are on Curtiss and Roosevelt Fields, within a short distance of each other, ready to take the air." The race was on.

All eyes were on Lindbergh. He was young, dashing, daring, and very shy. As photographers, well-wishers, and curiosity seekers crowded around him for attention, he focused on only one goal: to take off for Paris as quickly as possible. But the weather did not cooperate. Like his colleagues piloting the *America* and the *Columbia*, he, too, was dependent upon the respected professional advice of Doc Kimball. While the three crews waited, the planes were fine-tuned, checked, and rechecked. Proud representatives of the Wright Corporation hovered around each of the planes, offering a variety of services, technical and personal. No matter which plane flew first, it would be powered by a Wright Whirlwind engine.

Commander Byrd kept testing and retuning his plane and instruments and seemed in no particular hurry. Meanwhile, members of the *Columbia* camp continued their arguing. The rift between pilot Bertaud and owner Levine grew. The Brooklyn Chamber of Commerce stepped in to diffuse the situation by helping both sides draft a new contract that provided better financial terms and insurance benefits to the wives of both pilots. Levine grudgingly agreed to accept the terms, but a new contract was still not forthcoming. Bertaud was frustrated with the continued delays and feared that Levine, signed contract notwithstanding, might replace him with another pilot. The pilot's attorney obtained a court order against Levine preventing the *Columbia* from taking off without Bertaud as a pilot. A hearing was scheduled before a judge for May 20, 1927.

On May 19, as rain continued to fall, Charles A. Lindbergh headed into New York with friends for dinner and a Broadway show. With the flight constantly on his mind, he asked that his car be pulled over so that a telephone call could be made to Doc Kimball for the latest weather news. The meteorologist offered a glimmer of hope. Late reports from ships in the Atlantic showed a temporary break in the bad weather. Lindbergh quickly ordered the car to take him back to Curtiss Field. On the way he made one stop to pick up five sandwiches for the trip (two roast beef, two ham, and one egg salad). At the field he made

Three competitors

Before the first plane took off from Roosevelt Field, Charles A. Lindbergh (left) shakes hands with Clarence Chamberlin. Commander Richard E. Byrd is in the center. Behind them is the *Spirit of St. Louis.*

final arrangements for the plane's fueling and eventual ferrying to the adjacent Roosevelt Field and its longer runway. He then returned to his hotel for a few hours of sleep. By 3:00 a.m. he was back at his plane's hangar.

News of the impending flight reached the newsrooms of New York, and a small crowd of mechanics, police, reporters, photographers, and onlookers soon gathered in the rain. The tail of the *Spirit of St. Louis* was lashed to the back of a small truck and led by the group over a cleared path to Roosevelt Field. "It's more like a funeral procession than the beginning of a flight to Paris," Lindbergh later said.

At 7:54 a.m., May 20, 1927, as the *America* sat safely in its hangar and two court-ordered police officers stood guard over the *Columbia*, Charles A. Lindbergh rolled the heavily laden *Spirit of St. Louis* down the long runway. "A take-off seems hopeless," Lindbergh thought as the plane gathered speed along the seemingly endless runway. The plane headed for the runway's far edge. Onlookers held their collective breaths as Charles A. Lindbergh lifted the *Spirit of St. Louis* into the air and off into history.

3

LUCKY LINDY

"All I want in life is to throw myself down
flat, stretch out—and sleep."—Charles A. Lindbergh

What the pioneer aviators demonstrated in daring and bravery, they lacked in financial means. Transatlantic flights were expensive. Well-built airplanes, powered by the most reliable engines and outfitted with modern navigational aids, were well out of reach of most barnstormers. But it was not difficult for a resourceful flier to find wealthy backers. The country was in the midst of an economic boom in an exciting era—the Roaring Twenties—when headlines were full of the daring escapades of politicians, criminals, and aviators.

Commander Byrd, a famed explorer from a well-known family, had no problem in attracting a financial backer. Rodman Wanamaker, a wealthy department store owner and aviation buff, underwrote Byrd's attempt with a check for $100,000. Wanamaker leased Roosevelt Field for Byrd, paid for the airplane, and set out to grade the rough runway. The Orteig Prize meant nothing to both men. Wanamaker and Byrd approached the flight as a scientific experiment to demonstrate that long-distance aviation was not only possible but safe. The *New York Times* stated on March 3, 1927, that Wanamaker "does not wish the flight to be looked upon as a stunt, but as a distinct advance in long-distance flying."

The *Columbia* was owned by a self-made millionaire who, at first, thought a successful flight would benefit his business. In an attempt to obtain publicity for the flight, Charles Levine began to publicly announce conflicting plans of exactly who would fly the plane. In the ensuing confusion, bitter feuds erupted among Levine and his proposed pilots.

Charles A. Lindbergh was not a wealthy man. His father had been a congressman from Minnesota, and the family roots in the Midwest were firm and respected. During his barnstorming and airmail years, he managed to save a few thousand dollars. But more money was needed to fly the Atlantic. As he made plans for the flight, money became the crucial consideration.

On January 21, 1927, he sent a telegram to *Aviation and Aircraft* magazine requesting details of the Orteig Prize. He then approached a small group of aviation-minded St. Louis businessmen, who quickly raised $15,000 for Lindbergh's proposed flight. Any plane Lindbergh selected would be named the *Spirit of St. Louis* to give the investors' city positive publicity and a modern image.

Lindbergh contacted several aircraft manufacturers, but the plane he really wanted was the Wright-Bellanca. Its design was perfect for his needs. Giuseppe Bellanca had designed his plane to be the best-lifting airplane of its time. Unlike other potential transatlantic fliers, Lindbergh thought that a single-winged aircraft with one reliable engine would be better than a two-winged, multiengine craft. "Multiengined planes are more complicated," he told his doubting backers; "there are more things likely to go wrong with them. Besides, the greatest danger lies in weather, and in take-off with a full load—not in engine failure." The earlier crash of the heavily loaded Sikorsky plane made him realize that "a plane that's got to break the world's record for nonstop flying should be stripped of every excess ounce of weight." His concern with a plane's weight also influenced his desire to fly alone.

In November 1926, he traveled to the offices of the Wright Aeronautical Corporation in New Jersey and met the plane's designer, Giuseppe Bellanca. Although Bellanca was interested, the Wright Corporation, now focused only on building engines, was not, and Lindbergh turned to other sources.

On February 3, 1927, assured by the promised financial backing of the St. Louis businessmen, Lindbergh sent a telegram, signed by his employer at the time, Robertson Aircraft, to T. Claude Ryan, president of Ryan Airlines in San Diego, California. Lindbergh did not use his own name since no one knew who he was, he reasoned, and Ryan might not even respond. In the message, Lindbergh inquired if the company could build a plane to fly the Atlantic and how much it would cost. The following day, a reply telegram stated that Ryan could build such a plane in three months at a price of $6,000 plus the cost of an engine. Time was of the essence. Three months might be too long. In reply to another Lindbergh telegram, Ryan confidently responded, "Can complete in two months ..."

Meanwhile, a message from Bellanca urged Lindbergh to meet him in New York City. The young pilot's hopes rose. His first-choice plane might yet be available. Lindbergh took the train to New York to meet Charles A. Levine, the new owner of the Wright-Bellanca. "So you want to buy our Bellanca?" Levine asked. "Yes, sir," Lindbergh answered and proceeded to explain his dream of flying the Atlantic. "We would contribute to such a flight," Levine said and stated a price of $15,000, much lower than the plane's actual worth. Lindbergh, excited at the thought of being able to fly the Bellanca, returned immediately to St. Louis with the news. Within days, he made a return trip to New York with a $15,000 check from his backers in his pocket.

But Levine had added a surprise twist. "We will sell our plane, but of course we reserve the right to select the crew that flies it," he told the astonished aviator. "You understand," Levine added, "we cannot let just anybody pilot our airplane across the ocean." Dejected, Lindbergh returned to St. Louis. Now, there remained only the Ryan Company. Lindbergh, at his backers' insistence, quickly headed for San Diego.

What Lindbergh found in San Diego surprised and impressed him. Ryan Airlines was housed on the second floor of a converted fish-packing building, with many of the old odors still fresh. Inside he found a small group of dedicated people who were prepared not only to build a plane to specification but to do the best job possible. Without hesitation Lindbergh sent a telegram to his backers in St. Louis. "Recommend closing deal," he told them.

For two months, Lindbergh remained in San Diego to observe the building of his plane. There, he developed a close personal friendship with the Ryan engineer who designed the plane and the craftsmen who built it. In turn, the employees of Ryan Airlines were enthusiastic about their new friend and his

Assembling wing parts

The workers at Ryan Airlines worked diligently to build the *Spirit of St. Louis* quickly and efficiently. Their factory was located in a converted fish cannery.

Fitting the wing

Inside the Ryan factory, the *Spirit of St. Louis* takes shape as the wing is fitted onto the fuselage. The wing was then removed for separate transport to Dutch Flats.

The wing is lowered

Too big to take out of the second floor of the factory by regular means, the wing is lowered by a crane onto a waiting railroad boxcar and then onto the ground.

dream. "They're as anxious to build a plane that will fly to Paris as I am to fly it there." They worked night and day. "Why does this damn thing have to be so perfect?" one worker asked. "For two reasons," Lindbergh replied. "The first is I'm not a good swimmer!"

They did not have time to experiment on or test new techniques but used the best materials and technology available at the time. One Ryan engineer called the plane "a flying gas tank." Because Lindbergh insisted on saving weight, the engineers eliminated all nonessential systems and equipment. Knowing that he might be forced down in the Atlantic, Lindbergh bought a small inflatable raft he saw in a local store window.

Ready for testing

Just prior to its first fuel-load test, Ryan workers pose with the *Spirit of St. Louis*. Lindbergh is in the center, standing on a gasoline drum.

Lindbergh, unlike many other barnstorming aviators, avoided alcoholic beverages, tobacco, and swearing. He was shy, soft-spoken, and thoughtful. He was also extremely organized. During his two months in San Diego, he compiled lists of things to do and items to be carried on his flight. He bought ship's maps of the Atlantic on which he drew out his proposed route. When an engineer asked him, "Are you sure one pilot, alone, can make a flight like that? It's going to be something like forty hours in the air ...," Lindbergh, who was not actually sure of the distance his flight would take, bundled the engineer into a car and rode to the San Diego Public Library. There, they measured the route on a globe and concluded that the trip was about 3,600 miles. Even as preparations for the flight continued, the issue on everyone's mind was safety. Lindbergh's mother, far away in Detroit, Michigan, proud of her son yet concerned, wrote to put him at ease, "for the first time in my life I realize that Columbus also had a mother."

There were moments when Lindbergh thought his attempt might be in vain. News reports relayed the status of other competitors. On the East Coast, Commander Byrd and Davis and Wooster were busily conducting tests on their respective airplanes. Meanwhile, Chamberlin and Acosta broke the world's endurance record by keeping the Bellanca plane aloft more than fifty-one hours. When one of Lindbergh's financial backers asked, "Supposing one of the others manages it before you start, what will you do?" The intrepid young pilot, who had never flown more than five hundred miles at a stretch, responded, "In that case, I'll try something else" and began seriously thinking about a flight across the Pacific or even around the world.

As the proud and determined workers at Ryan Airlines raced against time to put the finishing touches on the *Spirit of St. Louis*, news of their competitors reached San Diego. On April 16, Byrd's *America* was damaged in a crash

First takeoff
The *Spirit of St. Louis* in its first test flight on April 28, 1927.

landing during a test. On April 24, the *Columbia* was slightly damaged during the landing with Levine's young daughter aboard. Two days later, Davis and Wooster were killed during a test takeoff in their *American Legion*.

Unsure of success, Lindbergh took off on May 10, 1927, for St. Louis, Missouri, on the first half of his trip to get his plane in position to fly the Atlantic. At the same time, newspapers reported conflicting news about the Nungesser and Coli flight from Paris. By the time he reached St. Louis, it was clear that the two French pilots were lost. With the *America* and the *Columbia* still on the ground in New York but ready to fly at any moment, Lindbergh was in a hurry to get there. After reaching St. Louis in record-breaking time, 14 hours and 25 minutes, he stayed only overnight and begged off from the dinner parties and social commitments arranged by his backers to take off for New York early on the morning of May 12.

What met him at Curtiss Field was worse than any crash landing he had ever experienced. It was the excited, noisy crowd, including jostling reporters and photographers who surrounded his airplane. "Each moment," he wrote, "I feel more uncomfortable. It's not like San Diego or St. Louis." All eyes were on the young, handsome, and unknown arrival. He became an overnight news sensation throughout the country.

Wright Aeronautical Corporation, whose engine powered the plane, came to Lindbergh's aid by providing public relations people to guide the inexperienced young man through the noisy mob of reporters. For a week, as bad weather kept all three planes on the ground, Lindbergh carefully supervised the mechanics who fine-tuned the *Spirit of St. Louis*. While he waited for the weather to clear, he watched for any imminent activity by his two competitors. He was also worried that he might have to forfeit the Orteig Prize by flying before the sixty-day waiting period expired. To reassure him, one of his backers said, "To hell with the money. When you're ready to take off, go ahead." At 7:54 on the morning of May 20, he did.

Lindbergh's concern with added weight dictated the number of items aboard. According to Lindbergh's own list, his supplies consisted of two flashlights, one ball of string, one ball of cord, one hunting knife, four red flares, one match safe (to keep matches dry), one large needle (the body of the plane was canvas), two canteens, one apparatus for making water from breath, one air raft, five cans of army emergency rations (to supplement the five sandwiches he bought on the way to the field), two air cushions (to float in the water), and one hacksaw blade. He was used to traveling light. Of his airmail flight days, he remembered, "We carried nothing but one emergency flare and a pocket flashlight."

The competition was initially discouraged as they watched Lindbergh take off. Giuseppe Bellanca said, "If Lindbergh makes it, there is no need for duplication." The *Columbia*'s owner, Charles A. Levine, was pessimistic about his own project. This young unknown had upstaged the *Columbia*. At the same time, the Post Office Department, after investigating Levine's finances, denied his company a valuable airmail-contract route between New York and Chicago. Bellanca was frustrated with Levine's behavior, and the long-standing feud between them led to Bellanca's severing business relations with Columbia Aircraft and Levine. The *Columbia*'s owner said huffily, "Due to Bellanca's resignation, the plane will be placed in the hangar and the New York to Paris flight will be abandoned for the present." He would soon have a change of heart. Byrd, seemingly unaffected by the actions in the other camps, continued his scientific testing program.

From the moment Lindbergh gingerly piloted the *Spirit of St. Louis* over the telephone poles at the end of the runway and disappeared from view, he became the center of world attention. At a boxing match that evening in New York's Yankee Stadium, the ring announcer relayed Lindbergh's latest position as forty thousand spectators rose in silent prayer for the young pilot's safety. Radio, then in its infancy, issued hourly reports, even when Lindbergh was out of sight over the Atlantic. People could only wonder what was happening and hope that everything would turn out well.

From the beginning, he looked upon his venture as a cooperative effort. His St. Louis backers, the people at Ryan Airlines, and the plane itself were all equal partners on the journey. To him, the *Spirit of St. Louis* was more a "living partner in adventure than a machine of cloth and steel." Indeed, on his return, he wrote a best-selling book about his flight, which he simply called *We*.

Lindbergh settled into his "little box with fabric walls" and took note of his surroundings. No aspect of the plane's construction had escaped his attention, not even the tubes that carried the precious fuel to the powerful Whirlwind engine. "[M]y plane and my life," he recalled, "depend on the slender stream of liquid flowing through them, like blood in human veins." He was assured. "Each dial and lever is in proper place for glance or touch; and the slightest pressure on controls brings response. My ears have become accustomed to the radial engine's tempo. It blends with the instrument readings and the clearing mist to instill a feeling of confidence and hope."

The first hours of flight brought Lindbergh over several bodies of seawater in between stretches of land. He flew over Long Island Sound, the water between Cape Cod and Nova Scotia, and finally, the sea between Nova Scotia and Newfoundland, all the while charting his position by landmarks on his map. Once past Newfoundland, there were no more familiar landmarks. Ahead lay the vast and desolate Atlantic. The next land he would see was in Europe.

Technically, everything was going well. But a major life-threatening problem began to develop. The pilot was getting sleepy. Lindbergh had anticipated this, and to help him stay awake during the flight, he had purposely prevented the Ryan Company from making adjustments that would increase the craft's stability. This would force him to pay more attention to the plane. He had told Ryan, "I don't plan on going to sleep while I fly." Yet conditions were not working out as planned. He had gotten little sleep over the previous twenty-four hours and now had to endure at least another thirty hours awake and alert.

He had fought with the Ryan engineers over the idea of an open cockpit. They finally compromised by placing windows on the plane but not installing them. During the flight, Lindbergh thought of putting them in to save fuel by cutting wind resistance but decided against it. "Windows would cut down the flow of air through my cockpit. ... They'd insulate me from a strength I'll need before my flight is done."

The *Spirit of St. Louis* cockpit

This view from the cockpit door shows the woven wicker seat and the control stick.

Instrument panel, the *Spirit of St. Louis*

Lindbergh sat behind what was a giant fuel tank. He had no forward and little side visibility. Note the periscope screen in the top center of the roof.

As he flew, his thoughts drifted back to his family and his childhood in Little Falls, Minnesota. He was always interested in mechanical and scientific experiments and liked to putter around the family home during summer vacations. He had traveled much and spent a great deal of time in Washington, D.C., with his father, the congressman, meeting the leading political figures of the time. Because of his family's schedule, he had "irregular" schooling. "Up to the time I entered the University of Wisconsin," he remembered, "I had never attended for one full school year. ..." Even at the university, he had difficulties and left midway through his second year to take flying lessons.

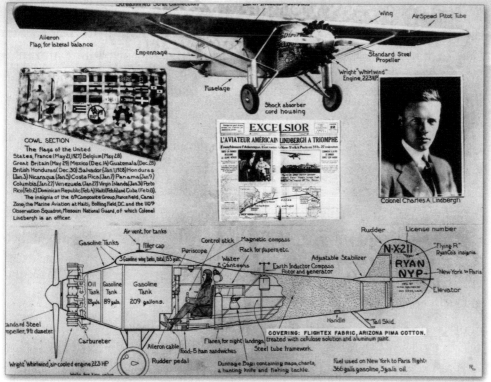

Composite photo of the *Spirit of St. Louis*

A cross section of the *Spirit of St. Louis* shows all the major parts labeled.

As the *Spirit of St. Louis* flew through the darkness, Lindbergh was aware only of the sound of the mighty Whirlwind engine that kept him in the air. "There's something in its rhythm that assures me, and gives me confidence with which to enter the unknown space ahead—to climb up over the fog, over the sea, and into the night." He maneuvered the *Spirit* through the clouds to bypass thunderheads. Sometimes he thought he saw mountains or the coasts of islands beneath his wings. Of course, they were only mirages, images of a tired mind. He heard voices from the past, advising him and reassuring him. They were friendly phantoms "able to vanish or appear at will, to pass in and out through the walls of the fuselage as though no walls were there." They gave him hope.

Now, as he flew through the darkness, fighting the urge to sleep, his thoughts turned to the barnstorming years before he enlisted in the Army Air Service. Details of his experiences flashed through his mind, almost lulling him into unconsciousness. Yet he fought to maintain the difference between dreams of his past and the reality of his present condition. "I'll continue on my course as long as engine can hold plane in air," he reasoned with himself.

He kept a log of his plane's statistical information—headings, fuel consumption, and speed. Hour after hour he continued flying in a near state of numbness. Finally, after twenty-six hours in the air, a strange movement in the water beneath his wing attracted his attention. It was a porpoise, the first sign of life he had seen since the North American continent. At first he thought it was just another mirage. Once he realized it wasn't, he began to engage in mental and flying exercises. He brought the plane down so the wheels almost touched the waves to see how close he could come. Then he repeated the exercise, sharpening his senses. Shortly thereafter he spotted some fishing boats. "Which way is Ireland?" he shouted as he flew low over a boat. No response. An hour later he saw the coast of Ireland. "I stare at it intently, not daring to believe my eyes ...," he recounted. Just knowing that he had safely crossed the Atlantic renewed his energy.

Reenergized and more alert, Lindbergh confidently flew toward the English Channel and Paris. As night covered the European continent, he crossed the coast of France in the thirty-second hour of flight. An hour later he circled the Eiffel Tower. News of his positions flashed around the world. In Paris, citizens crowded into automobiles and set out to Le Bourget Airfield to greet the daring young American.

At first, the lights on the ground below confused the pilot. He thought they might be from factories in the area of the field. As he landed, he suddenly realized the lights came from the thousands of automobiles choking every road leading to the airport. Lindbergh carefully landed the *Spirit of St. Louis* at Le Bourget at 10:22 p.m. (French time), May 21, 1927, 33 hours and 30 minutes after leaving New York, well within the projected forty-hour time frame.

In the glare of the floodlights, Lindbergh saw thousands of people running toward him. His New York reception upon arrival at Roosevelt Field had been frightening; Paris was unbelievable! He quickly cut the engine to stop the propeller. He was afraid the whirling blade would kill someone. Within moments, the *Spirit of St. Louis* was surrounded by a shouting, animated crowd of well-wishers who literally scooped the dazed young pilot out of the cockpit and passed him around on their shoulders. "For nearly half an hour," he recalled, "I was unable to touch the ground." Their cheers were deafening. The shy young man, who just days earlier was an unknown airmail pilot from the American Midwest, had instantly become the world's most famous person by safely flying 3,610 miles across the Atlantic in 33 hours and 30 minutes.

4

"WELL, HERE WE ARE."

"I am very happy."
—Charles A. Lindbergh

Charles A. Lindbergh thought he had planned every aspect of his flight. Before leaving New York, he even secured a letter of introduction to French authorities. The twenty-five-year-old pilot reasoned that he knew no one in Paris. The crowds at Le Bourget overwhelmed him. From that moment until the day he died, Lindbergh would never go anywhere unnoticed.

Leaving the airfield with his body intact became Lindbergh's first challenge in Paris. When the plane came to a stop, the young pilot stared at the onrushing

The *Spirit of St. Louis* lands
French police and soldiers surround the *Spirit of St. Louis* to protect it from the hordes of excited people gathered at Le Bourget to welcome Lindbergh to France.

horde. As he stepped out of the cockpit, two police officers offered help. "Oh, you don't have to help me out," Lindbergh said, and he jumped to the ground.

The uncontrollable crowds grabbed at him, lifted him high in the air, and cheered deliriously. Two alert French fliers, fearing imminent personal danger to the young American, snatched Lindbergh's helmet off his head and placed it squarely on a nearby American reporter. The crowd, not knowing who was who, instantly turned its attention toward the unfortunate reporter, giving Lindbergh an opportunity to slip unnoticed into a hangar. There, he was rescued by the American ambassador, Myron T. Herrick.

With only a few dollars in his pocket and not even a change of clothes, Lindbergh was unprepared for the receptions, diplomatic dinners, and royal audiences that awaited him in Europe. Gratefully, the young man accepted the hospitality and guidance of Ambassador Herrick and the American Embassy staff.

Parisians wait for their hero

Thousands crowd in front of a Paris hotel, waiting for Lindbergh to emerge following a luncheon.

From the moment he landed, the young flier enchanted the French people. They were particularly impressed when Lindbergh telephoned his mother across the Atlantic with news of his safe arrival—not an easy thing to arrange in 1927. The French were also touched when the successful flier visited Madame Nungesser, mother of the much loved and now mourned French pilot whose flight had ended in his disappearance. The grieving mother tearfully told Lindbergh, "You are a very brave young man. I congratulate you from the bottom of my heart. I, too, have a brave son, who I have never ceased to believe is still fighting his way back to civilization."

In borrowed suits and formal wear, the shy hero became the honored guest of the French people. No matter how much praise he received, he spoke not of his own personal triumph but of the future of aviation. At the American Club in Paris he stated that his flight "demonstrate[d] the reliability of the commercial motors today and the trip itself the practicality of transatlantic flying ..."

Lindbergh waves to Paris crowd
From the balcony of the American Embassy, Lindbergh greets thousands of well-wishers. This is a photo wired to newspapers in the United States.

In a rousing appearance before the Chamber of Deputies, he told lawmakers that aviation would "bring our peoples nearer together in understanding and in friendship than they have ever been." People wanted to see him, touch him, and feel they somehow were part of this great moment in history. He visited Napoleon's tomb, received the Legion of Honor medal from Gaston Doumergue, the president of France, and was the guest of honor at an official state banquet held in a hangar at Le Bourget with the *Spirit of St. Louis* as the centerpiece.

Decorated with the Legion of Honor

Charles Lindbergh was decorated with the Legion of Honor by French president Gaston Doumergue. On the right is United States ambassador Myron Herrick.

In a poignant meeting, Lindbergh was introduced to the aging Louis Blériot, the aviation pioneer who had made the sensational flight eighteen years earlier across the English Channel. "I shall always regard you as my master," the young American graciously said. "Ah, but you, my son," the aviation legend said, "are the prophet of a new era when flying will be as common as motor steamship traffic is today."

With the legendary aviator Louis Blériot

Lindbergh had an emotional meeting with Blériot, the first man to fly across the English Channel.

Wherever he went, cheering crowds followed. On May 26 the city of Paris held its official reception. Half a million people thronged the streets to catch a glimpse of Lindbergh as he was presented with yet another gold medal. True to form, the modest pilot responded to the honor by predicting the start of regular air service between the United States and France. People in the crowd roared

Lindbergh in Paris

Lindbergh is shown in front of the United States Embassy with American ambassador Myron Herrick.

their approval. When he paid tribute to the memories of Nungesser and Coli, some in the crowd openly wept.

Across the Atlantic, Americans were equally excited. During the time Lindbergh was in the air, the telephone switchboard at the *New York Times* was overwhelmed by ten thousand callers inquiring about his progress and safety. Within moments of learning that he had made it safely across to Paris, shrieking fire whistles, clanging bells, and shouts of joy echoed throughout the land in celebration. People all over the country were eager to welcome Lindbergh home and show national pride for his accomplishment.

In Washington, government leaders recognized the sudden emergence of

Lindbergh as a valuable folk hero. President Coolidge sent a congratulatory telegram to Lindbergh, promoting him instantly from the rank of captain to colonel in the U.S. Army Air Corps Reserve. In addition, the president ordered the U.S. cruiser *Memphis* to return Lindbergh and the *Spirit of St. Louis* to the United States from France with the greatest possible speed. America prepared to welcome home Lindbergh as no hero had ever been welcomed before.

In Europe, Lindbergh had a few more stops remaining on his itinerary. On May 28, Lindbergh piloted the *Spirit* from Paris to Brussels, Belgium. In a last tribute to Paris, he flew low over the cheering crowds, performing "aerial gymnastics." The crowds in Brussels, more orderly than in France, greeted him with equal warmth as an air hero and as an American. The United States, after all, had helped liberate that country from German occupation during the Great War. King Albert decorated him with yet another medal.

From Brussels, he flew to a rousing welcome in London, England, which he later described as "worse than I had in Paris." He had to climb an airport tower to escape the excited crowd. When he arrived at the American Embassy, 150,000 cheering people milled around the building.

In London, he participated in another round of luncheons, dinners, and royal receptions. The British Air Council presented him with the *Daily Mail*'s Aviation Cup. He was received at Buckingham Palace by King George V and later spoke privately with Edward, the Prince of Wales. "What [are you] going to do in the future?" the prince asked. "I am going to keep on flying," Lindbergh answered.

At a formal banquet in his honor given by British reporters, Lindbergh found the plate before him filled with five sandwiches and a half-gallon of water. To everyone's amusement, his host announced, "Captain Lindbergh will now partake of his customary meal."

Lindbergh then flew back to France, and the *Spirit of St. Louis* was crated for shipment back to the United States. The U.S. cruiser *Memphis*, with pilot and plane onboard, departed France on June 4. The seven-day voyage offered a little opportunity for rest and relaxation. Lindbergh toured the ship, met with the crew, and was interviewed by reporters onboard. To honor a commitment made before the flight, he wrote a daily report for the *New York Times*, which was radioed back to land for eager readers.

On Saturday, June 11, the *Memphis* sailed up Chesapeake Bay to dock at the Navy Yard in Washington, D.C. The cruiser was accompanied part of the way by an escort of four destroyers, forty airplanes, and two blimps. On the dock stood a welcoming committee that included Washington's most influential people, including nearly all the members of the president's cabinet. The first person escorted up the gangplank to greet Lindbergh was his mother. From early morning, people gathered along the announced parade route, and all official business in the capital came to a halt.

Lindbergh with his mother

Lindbergh and his mother are shown in an open car during a parade in his honor in Washington, D.C.

Lindbergh addresses nation

Charles Lindbergh speaks to the nation at an official reception in Washington on June 11, 1927. He was introduced by President Calvin Coolidge, who awarded him the Distinguished Flying Cross medal.

At the Washington Monument, 250,000 people crowded around the specially built platform, and millions more around the country tuned in their radios at home to hear a rare live broadcast of a special ceremony. President Coolidge, never a lengthy speaker, delivered a stirring oration on America's preeminent role in aviation and presented Lindbergh with the Distinguished Flying Cross. The young flier responded with characteristic brief words, "I bring a message home to you ... the affection of the people of France for the people of America. ..."

But nothing Lindbergh had experienced since his arrival in France could have prepared him for the greeting that awaited him in New York. On Monday morning, June 13, he flew from Washington to Long Island on a borrowed plane.

Millions cheered
Part of a crowd of thousands who gathered on the Mall in Washington, D.C., to greet Lindbergh.

New York reception for Lindbergh

Over five hundred vessels jam the harbor to welcome Lindbergh home. He is onboard the *Macom*, the official yacht of the city of New York (the larger white ship at bottom left and close to fireboats).

The *Spirit of St. Louis* remained behind in Washington for needed repairs. He transferred to an amphibious plane at Mitchel Field and landed in the water in New York's lower harbor. There he boarded the city's official yacht, the *Macom*. Accompanied by an armada of five hundred ships of various types and sizes and the din of ships' whistles, horns, and bells, the *Macom* sailed up the harbor to the Battery at the southernmost tip of Manhattan.

Lindbergh took his place in an open car next to New York's popular mayor, James J. Walker. It was estimated that 4.5 million people lined the streets of New York that day to catch a glimpse of Lindbergh. The parade honoring him took five hours. Bands marched, thousands of flags waved, and tons of confetti and ticker tape fell like snow from the open windows of the city's skyscrapers. In a radio first, millions more throughout the country sat before their sets to hear live details of the parade from reporters strategically placed along the route. It was the first time that multiple radio reporters covered a historic event.

At City Hall, Mayor Walker presented Lindbergh with a medal and the key to the city. "I don't give it to you," the mayor said, "you won it." At Central Park, 300,000 people awaited Lindbergh's arrival, including New York's governor, Alfred E. Smith. For four days, the young hero was feted at banquets, dinners, and receptions. Wherever he appeared, crowds gathered to share in the happiness. In Brooklyn, more than one million turned out.

On June 16, he formally received the $25,000 Orteig Prize and the medal that went with it. That evening, after a dinner on Rodman Wanamaker's yacht, he slipped away at 1:30 a.m. to Mitchel Field. There, he borrowed a flying helmet and an airplane and flew back to Washington to retrieve his own plane. By 7:30 a.m. on Friday morning, he was back in New York with the *Spirit*, prepared to take off again an hour later for the flight's namesake city, St. Louis. On the way, he flew over the Wright Aeronautical plant in Paterson, New Jersey, in tribute to the J-5 Whirlwind engine that had made his flight possible.

From July 20 to October 23, Lindbergh flew the *Spirit of St. Louis* on a highly publicized national tour that covered eighty-two stops in all forty-eight states, a total of 22,000 miles. Schools were dismissed and thousands lined the streets to catch a glimpse of the new American hero. In his tour of the United States and later visits to Canada and Mexico, Lindbergh received thousands of gifts from national leaders and ordinary citizens. During 1928, the first year that his medals, trophies, symbolic keys to cities, and priceless jewelry were displayed at the Missouri Historical Society, more than 2.5 million people came to visit. In the months following Lindbergh's triumphant homecoming, the country was inundated with memorabilia honoring the pilot, including toys, puzzles, wallpaper, games, and replicas of the *Spirit of St. Louis*. Songs and poems were written about his bravery, idealism, and patriotism. The poems were reprinted in newspapers and magazines, the songs heard by millions over the radio or played on their home record players. Hundreds of songs about Lindbergh were written. While "Lucky Lindy" was perhaps the most popular, other titles included "Won't You Take Me to Heaven, Please, Lucky Lindy Do" and "Just Like a Butterfly through Sun and Rain." Many families named their new baby sons *Charles Lindbergh* as tribute to the famous pilot.

At a time when a leading United States senator received money for endorsing Lucky Strike cigarettes in newspapers ads, Lindbergh never endorsed products for payment. That did not prevent some companies from using his name. In the week following the flight, the Mobil Oil Company proudly told newspaper readers that "Lindbergh uses Gargoyle Mobiloil in his thrilling airplane leap across the Atlantic." The Waterman Pen Company informed people that Lindbergh had taken one of its pens on the *Spirit*.

Lindbergh received hundreds of business offers, including a lucrative film contract. He turned them all down. One offer that he did not refuse was to write a book for G. P. Putnam's publishing house. The book, modestly called *We*, was written in three weeks and became an international best seller.

Almost forgotten in the national hysteria over Lindbergh were the two remaining pilots still at Roosevelt and Curtiss fields. Commander Byrd would not be hurried from his laborious testing program with the *America*. He wished Lindbergh well and was genuinely pleased with the young man's success. Byrd told reporters that Lindbergh was "a super hero who has carried high the banner of American spirit." Byrd viewed his own mission as more than a one-time, single-engine flight. His three-engined *America* was designed as the forerunner of a regular airline service between the United States and France. The time-consuming testing continued, with no takeoff date in sight as Byrd kept analyzing the data.

News of Lindbergh's success was more upsetting for Charles Levine and Clarence Chamberlin, who both issued congratulatory statements about their rival's success. They had been frustrated to learn that the injunction against the *Columbia* was lifted on the very day Lindbergh took off for Paris, May 20. Levine fired Lloyd Bertaud, leaving Chamberlin as the only pilot. A new round of public speculation arose concerning the identity of the second crew member. Disappointed that he was not first across, Levine angrily ordered workers to paint over the word *Paris* on the *Columbia*'s side. The plane's new destination became another matter of public curiosity as the guessing game intensified. When Bellanca, upset at Levine's antics and the delays that prevented his plane from being first, announced his resignation from Columbia Aircraft, Levine then insisted that Bellanca's name on the plane's rudder be covered with paint as well.

Still angry, Levine stated, "The plane will be placed in the hangar. Mr. Bellanca's resignation causes us to abandon plans for the New York–Paris flight for the present." Despite what had happened, work still continued on the *Columbia*. Levine went up with Chamberlin on test runs, during which the experienced aviator gave the owner basic flying lessons. On the ground, Chamberlin directed preparations for an eventual transatlantic flight to a yet unnamed destination with a yet unnamed second pilot.

Although Lindbergh had won the race, public excitement about future flights continued. While everyone waited for the next takeoffs, pilots at Curtiss Field kept busy by offering popular fifteen-minute sightseeing rides over Long Island. More than five hundred daring people paid to go up in the air during the weekend following Lindbergh's flight. It was not long before the world's attention was focused on another plane.

5

"TO BERLIN! TO BERLIN!"

"We had plenty of luck, only it was all hard."
—Charles A. Levine

Grace Levine could not believe it. The airplane was about to take off and her husband, dressed in a business suit, was still calmly sitting with Clarence Chamberlin in the cockpit. She had promised to burn the plane if he even thought of going on this flight. Now, there was Charles A. Levine, looking straight ahead, not daring even a sideways glance at his wife, who was frantically shouting, "Oh-h-h! He's not going? He's not going?"

It was 6:00 a.m. on Saturday, June 4, and hundreds of reporters and curious citizens were crowded onto Roosevelt Field. The plane headed down the runway, but the crush of people on the strip forced the plane back. The *Columbia*'s chief mechanic, John Carisi, reassured Mrs. Levine that her husband was merely testing the plane with Chamberlin. As the aircraft came to a stop, Carisi jumped onto the plane and spoke to Levine. "What are you up to, Mr. Levine? I must say you gave us all a shock. Your wife's quite upset: she thought you were going to fly to Europe." Everyone in the crowd still awaited the expected arrival of the surprise second pilot Levine had promised. Levine pushed the mechanic off the plane as it turned around quickly and headed down the runway a second time.

Charles A. Levine may have been nervous about his wife's reaction, but he owned this airplane and he was definitely going. To the cheers of thousands who had come to witness the historic moment, the plane lumbered down the runway and was quickly airborne. Mrs. Levine fainted.

The plane was loaded with as much fuel as it could hold. It was so heavy that it barely cleared the end of the long runway at Roosevelt Field, where Commander Byrd's plane, the *America*, waited for its time to fly.

Once aloft, Levine changed into a flight suit that he had stored onboard earlier. Although it seemed impossible to the people on the ground, there could be no doubt now as to who the second pilot was. Among the supplies were two vacuum bottles filled with chicken soup, ten chicken sandwiches, army emergency rations and a rubber raft (but no oars). Chamberlin later told an angry Levine that he didn't take oars because "it would be too far to row back." For the first hundred miles, the flight went perfectly. Then Chamberlin and Levine noticed that their new and expensive earth inductor compass was not working properly. Instruments sometimes behaved erratically on long flights because of

The *Columbia* in flight
This photo was taken during the *Columbia*'s record-breaking flight over Roosevelt Field, New York.

The *America's* ground crew

Each of the three planes depended on the skills and knowledge of dedicated workers. Without them, the pilots could not have succeeded.

the constant vibration, so John Carisi had tried to overcome that problem by suspending the entire instrument panel in rubber shock absorbers, but with minimal success.

As strong headwinds blew the plane off course, they knew they would have to depend on the less reliable magnetic compass onboard. They briefly considered turning back but Levine, perhaps thinking of his wife's anger at his going, calmly told Chamberlin, "I'd rather be in Davy Jones' locker [the bottom of the sea, the resting place of drowned sailors] than go back and face those newspapermen."

Using flight-plan charts developed by Bernt Balchen, a member of the *America's* crew, Chamberlin guided the *Columbia* on a course over Nova Scotia and, at 6:20 that evening, out to the open sea beyond the islands of St.-Pierre and Miquelon. Balchen was an accomplished navigator and "sat up one night with Chamberlin in the Garden City Hotel until midnight to plot a course for the *Columbia*." When Byrd later asked Chamberlin what system of navigation he had used, the *Columbia*'s pilot answered, "Well, Admiral, I used Balchen's system, and figured I couldn't miss Europe." "This part of the trip was a dream of beauty," they later wrote. "Visibility was so good that we could see fifty to a hundred miles." As they took one last look at the North American continent near Cape Race on the tip of Newfoundland, Levine prophetically turned to Chamberlin and said, "Europe next stop. Well, here goes nothing." Their mission was to fly as far into Europe as their fuel capacity would allow. Chamberlin later revealed, "I was not at all sure where we should come out on the other side."

After passing Newfoundland, they saw ships beneath them in the darkness. Levine held his flashlight out the window and was comforted by a return flash of light. "She'll give a report on us," he reassured Chamberlin. A short time later the fliers encountered a dense fog, which required them to lift the plane to 15,000 feet. Before leaving New York, the pilot had asked Doc Kimball what to expect over the Atlantic. The weather forecaster answered, "You want to know what the weather is going to be 4,000 miles away and 48 hours in advance? I can't tell you for sure whether it's going to rain here tomorrow." The *Columbia* was not equipped with instruments for "blind" flying—the ability to "see" through thick fog and rain. Chamberlin later said that instruments onboard didn't matter to him. "I didn't know how to use them anyway, because I never learned to fly by instruments for the same reason that I never learned how to milk a cow: for fear that I might have to do it some day."

The darkness that enveloped them only highlighted how alone they both were. Sleep was impossible. "You get so accustomed to listening to the roaring of the motor that your ear gets trained to every beat," Chamberlin later wrote. "If it is missing," he continued, "the plane would drop to the ocean—or the ground—where death may await you." Chamberlin occupied himself with keeping the plane on course. Levine thought of his family. Writing later in the *New York Times*, he recalled telling Chamberlin—perhaps just a bit dramatically, "My daughter, Eloyse, is going to bed at home many hundred miles westward ... asking God to get daddy over there safely, and her mother joining her in the prayer and perhaps crying."

As they flew on into the night, the outside temperature at 15,000 feet hovered at the freezing point, and the plane's windshield began icing up. "We'll have to get out of this quick!" Chamberlin shouted and maneuvered the plane into a fast, dangerous dive. As the plane descended sharply toward the water and warmer temperatures, the ice began melting. When Chamberlin finally leveled the plane off at 500 feet, they found themselves flying into calmer and clearer weather. They celebrated their close escape from death with a breakfast of chicken soup, oranges, and coffee.

On they flew, unaware of their exact position. At 11:30 a.m. their spirits lifted when they caught sight of a large passenger ship. "She appeared to have sprung out of the sea by magic," Chamberlin recalled. Flying low, they circled the ship at 150 feet to read the ship's name on the bow: RMS *Mauretania*. Passengers ran to the railings, waved, and threw hats and books wildly into the air. In return, the two fliers waved back. To make certain the ship's officers would radio the *Columbia*'s position, Levine stuck his hands out an open window and imitated a telegraph operator tapping out signals. An officer signaled his understanding and radioed the aircraft's position to New York. Levine then had an idea. He pulled out a copy of the previous day's *New York Times* and turned to the shipping page. By pinpointing the precise time the *Mauretania* had left the French port of Cherbourg and by estimating the ship's speed, the fliers determined they were approximately 350 miles from Europe.

"I want to go where he [the *Mauretania*] came from," Chamberlin thought. "So I got out in front, flew down the middle of the ship," set the magnetic compass to that course, and flew on securely toward Europe. "Where are you taking me, anyway—to Berlin or Rome?" Levine asked. Chamberlin responded jokingly, "Maybe Spain or Africa, you never can tell. Your guess is as good as mine. ..." Their intended destination was Berlin, but because Lindbergh had been the first to get to Paris, their new goal was simply to "fly farther than anyone else had ever flown without stopping." Speculation by reporters also focused on such cities as Vilnius, Lithuania, and Warsaw, Poland.

The report from the *Mauretania* eased Grace Levine's concern. Confident that Germany was the *Columbia*'s ultimate destination, she sent a telegram to her husband in care of the American ambassador in Berlin. "Following your flight with prayer, love, pride, and confidence. Love from family. Cable promptly. Will leave to meet you." Levine's father, Isaac, was even more enthusiastic. When reporters asked him what he thought of his son's flight, he proudly said, "Charlie's is a greater feat than Lindbergh's!" When asked to explain his remark, he continued, "Well, it's Lindbergh's business to fly. He sort of had to go. But Charlie didn't have to go. He just went!"

Chamberlin's wife told reporters, "How I wish I'd been aboard that ship! I can see him leaning out, and waving to all those people." His mother said, "I'm not worried in the least. I was worried before he left, but not now!" A special ceremony was held by the Brooklyn Chamber of Commerce to honor the fliers' wives, and the German government invited the women to travel to Germany onboard the liner *Berlin*.

Thirty minutes after circling the *Mauretania*, Chamberlin and Levine spotted another ship off in the distance. They flew low and identified it as the U.S. cruiser *Memphis*, carrying the triumphant Lindbergh and the *Spirit of St. Louis* back to America. "Levine wanted me to fly over and 'jazz her up' ...," Chamberlin recalled. But time and fuel were wasting away, and the *Columbia* continued on toward Europe. Lindbergh wrote later in his report to the *New York Times* that he was "naturally disappointed that the *Memphis* did not sight the plane, for it would have been a great thrill for me to see the plane attempting the same flight I made."

Toward dusk, the tired fliers caught their first sight of Europe as the *Columbia* flew over Land's End on England's southwestern tip. They gazed down with relief and satisfaction as the plane flew over the lush green countryside. Their initial joy soon faded to anxiety as they had to climb higher and higher to escape massive cloud formations to cross the English Channel toward the Continent.

The plane was on a direct course for Germany, and its progress was relayed by radio throughout Europe. Lights at London's Croydon Airfield were kept on all night in the event that bad weather forced the *Columbia* to land there. In Germany, air and police forces were mobilized and searchlights began scouring the air. The *New York Times* reported that, as during the Lindbergh flight, its telephone switchboard was flooded with thousands of calls from people inquiring about the *Columbia*. Among the callers were Giuseppe Bellanca and Commander Richard Byrd.

No matter how high Chamberlin and Levine climbed, they could not escape the clouds and fog. Chamberlin later said, "There was nothing more awe-inspiring, nothing more uncanny on the entire trip than the hours during which we were flying through dense masses of fog, often absolutely unaware where we might be or what we might strike at the next moment." It was night and Chamberlin decided to circle until dawn before resuming course.

Both men were near exhaustion at this point. Lack of sleep and the effects of high altitude and oxygen deprivation affected their minds and bodies. Chamberlin, desperately tired, turned the controls over to Levine. "See what you can do with her for a while; I've got to get some rest," Chamberlin said. The pilot stretched out on the shelf that formed the top of the gas tank (the plane was originally outfitted with six seats, four of which were removed for this flight and replaced with a huge fuel tank) and instantly fell asleep.

Within minutes he was startled awake. Something was dramatically wrong. The *Columbia* was spiraling toward the ground at high speed. Levine had stalled out the engine trying to climb above the clouds. Chamberlin clambered hastily to his seat and took control of the plane. In what seemed like a lifetime, he managed to gently coax the *Columbia* out of a three-mile death spiral and leveled the plane off at 4,000 feet. Chamberlin was emotionally drained by the frightening experience. The fearless Levine thought it was all good fun: like being on a "bucking bronco."

The plane, still surrounded by fog, maintained its easterly course. Chamberlin calculated that they must be somewhere over Germany. A little after 4:00 a.m. on June 6, he took the plane down to 1,000 feet. Ahead, the glare of flames reflected in the low-hanging fog encouraged them. "They're blast furnaces,"

Chamberlin said. "But where?" Levine asked. They circled the area trying to discover their location. Suddenly, they caught sight of white flares being shot up in the air. "That's for us," Chamberlin said. They flew toward the flares and discovered an airport. They later learned they were flying over Dortmund, Germany. Men on the ground waved at them. Chamberlin quieted the Whirlwind engine and glided the *Columbia* silently over the field at about 20 feet off the ground. He stuck his head out of the window and yelled at the men in his best high-school German, "*Nach Berlin? Nach Berlin?*" (To Berlin? To Berlin?) The men on the ground all pointed in the same direction. Chamberlin fired up the engine and headed off toward Berlin.

The only remaining question was whether there was enough fuel onboard to make it to Berlin. The *Columbia* did not have a gas gauge. Chamberlin confidently told a reporter that he could tell the gas level by simply rapping on the tank. Using that method, he began to realize that they were nearly out of fuel. Still, Levine was not prepared to land and urged Chamberlin to fly on as far as he could. "You're the doctor," Chamberlin told Levine. "It's your airplane, but it's brought us a long way and I'd hate to bend it up trying to make four or five extra miles." On they flew.

The two fliers still did not know how close they were to Berlin when the gas ran out shortly before 6:00 a.m. and the powerful Whirlwind engine sputtered and died. After reliably flying the *Columbia* 3,905 miles in almost 43 hours, Chamberlin glided to a rough landing in a wheat field near Eisleben, Germany, 108 miles from their destination. With no one in sight, the tired but elated fliers stretched their legs on German soil and rejoiced in their success. They had safely landed, breaking Lindbergh's distance record by 295 miles.

6

"FAR ENOUGH!"

"We have come from New York."
—Charles A. Levine

The welcome Chamberlin and Levine received in Germany was dramatically different from the one Lindbergh had received in France only days earlier. The *Columbia*'s pilots stood alone in the early morning mist, not quite sure where they were. Levine had forgotten to bring maps with him from New York. The local farmers who eventually arrived to work in the field were not initially friendly. The plane had damaged their wheat field, and the two fliers, unshaven and unkempt after their long journey, were mistaken for kidnappers. The farmers also found it difficult to believe that the two strangers came from New York. Once they realized that the men before them had just flown across the Atlantic, smiles and good spirits prevailed.

Through the use of hand motions and a few German words, Levine communicated their need for fuel. A boy headed off on a bike for the four-mile trip to town. A short while later, twenty gallons of gasoline arrived on a horse-drawn cart. The pilots next faced the problem of how to get the fuel into the plane's tank. A woman walked back to her home—a mile away—and returned with a teapot with a long, curved spout. It took Chamberlin an hour and a half to transfer the fuel to the plane—filling the teapot many times over. The pilots found a large piece of brown wrapping paper in the plane and wrote out a certificate describing the specifics of their landing. Then they asked the farmers to sign the paper as witnesses.

The pilots paid their new friends fifteen dollars for the fuel and said good-bye.

Levine climbed into the cockpit, ready to flick the starter switch at Chamberlin's command. Over and over, Chamberlin whirled the propeller and shouted, "Contact!" and "Switch off" until the engine finally caught. At 9:35 a.m. the two pilots took off for Berlin. Still without a map of Germany, they could only hope that the farmers had pointed them in the right direction.

In the air, both men began arguing about the plane's course. To complicate matters, the weather again turned foggy. "We didn't see how we could miss a city the size of Berlin," Chamberlin later said. But miss it they did. While Berlin—alerted by telephone that the *Columbia* was on its way—was preparing an appropriate welcome for the hero pilots, the plane was well east of the capital city and again running out of gas.

They flew over an airport, which they identified by the sign on a hangar roof, Cottbus. Without a map they had no way of knowing they were still sixty miles southeast from Berlin. They did know they needed to find a place to land. Ahead, they saw nothing but swamp. As the plane swung back to Cottbus, the engine sputtered and quit. Chamberlin quickly sent Levine to stand behind the gas tank to provide weight in the rear of the plane and prevent it from flipping over. On landing, the wheels dragged through the muddy field, creating furrows. The aircraft came to an abrupt stop when its nose tilted sharply forward into the ground, snapping the propeller.

To add insult to injury, powdered milk and cocoa, stored in the cockpit, spilled all over Chamberlin, giving him the appearance of a chocolate ghost. As the two pilots climbed out of their plane, Levine asked Chamberlin, "Are you all right, Clarence? Did you hurt yourself?" Chamberlin could only offer an apology. "I'm sorry, but I guess I broke the prop. It looks like we're all through flying." Levine sincerely replied, "Damn the prop. I was afraid something had happened to you. We've flown far enough for a while anyway."

A curious crowd began to assemble, but the officious mayor of Cottbus soon had the situation under control. He placed guards around the plane, arranged for it to be righted, and took charge of the two fliers. He escorted the tired and grimy Americans directly to a hotel, where delicious meals, hot

Landing in Cottbus
The *Columbia*'s landing in the muddy wheat field caused it to flip.

baths, and clean beds waited. The exhausted pilots slept for twelve hours. A *New York Times* reporter who rushed to Cottbus from Berlin described the event to his readers in a flowery manner. "Their sleep is sound and happy because they carried through to completion today one of the most splendid enterprises ever achieved by man on land or sea or in the air."

News of the emergency landing in Cottbus was flashed to Berlin, and the welcoming party waiting patiently at the city's Tempelhof Airfield disbanded. While the two pilots slept, a delegation of government officials, reporters, and a high-ranking diplomat from the American Embassy flew into Cottbus in a hastily assembled fleet of planes.

Cottbus basked in glory at the world attention. Chamberlin and Levine were wined, dined, serenaded, and honored during their stay as no previous visitors had been in the city's one-thousand-year history.

The *Columbia* in Germany

The *Columbia* stands on the Cottbus field where it landed after running out of fuel on June 6, 1927. The plane is shown after being righted from its landing position in which the propeller was broken.

When the pilots awoke the morning after their arrival, thousands of people had already gathered outside their hotel. After a rather hectic breakfast, during which autograph seekers and well-wishers managed to push through the police cordon, Chamberlin and Levine were escorted through the streets of Cottbus to city hall.

Awaiting them was the town band that repeatedly played a mangled version of "The Star Spangled Banner." A handmade American flag with fewer than the required number of stars fluttered proudly. After several official speeches, during which the fliers were showered with gifts and souvenirs, the mayor made Levine and Chamberlin honorary citizens of Cottbus. They were guaranteed the lifetime privilege of living in the town free of charge. Both were invited to return in 1930 to help the town celebrate its one-thousandth birthday. When the Nazis came to power in 1933 and instituted anti-Semitic laws, the Cottbus town council unceremoniously withdrew Levine's citizenship because he was Jewish.

Levine and Chamberlin in Germany
Their successful flight beat Lindbergh's distance record.

The authorities insisted on flying the two pilots to Berlin on a plane of the German airline, Lufthansa. Chamberlin and Levine firmly protested. Their original goal was to fly the *Columbia* to Berlin, and that's what they were going to do! When the ceremonies ended, Levine and Chamberlin went to a nearby soccer field where the *Columbia* had been towed. German technicians replaced the broken propeller with one brought from Berlin and refilled the fuel tank. While Levine remained on the ground, Chamberlin took the *Columbia* up for a test spin. Everything was fine. He flew the plane back to the Cottbus airfield, where Levine and his escorts met him.

After a friendly luncheon with the mayor and other town officials, the two pilots returned to the airfield. They were overcome by the outpouring of

Close-up of the *Columbia*

Note the destination city covered over with paint on the fuselage.

friendship and the effects of a heavy meal lubricated with good German beer. Accompanied by an escort of German planes, Chamberlin and Levine left Cottbus at 4:30 p.m. on June 7 for Berlin. There was no chance now they could miss the city.

Arriving early, before the official reception committee at the airfield had time to assemble, the *Columbia* and its flying escorts circled lazily over Berlin. People on the ground were delighted. By the time the plane landed at 6:30 p.m., one hundred thousand eager Germans had gathered at the Tempelhof Airfield while thousands more lined the route into the city.

The American ambassador, Jacob Schurman, was first to officially greet the fliers. "The American people are proud of you," he told them. He then extended the hospitality of the embassy and its staff to the heroes. A wreath of laurel leaves was placed on the plane's propeller while onlookers cheered and tossed flowers at the fliers. Along the motorcade route to the embassy, thousands more enthusiastically welcomed the Americans to Berlin. The crowds at the embassy

German police hold back crowds

Frenzied Germans greet Chamberlin and Levine on their arrival in Berlin.

would not disperse until the two fliers finally appeared on the balcony.

The next morning, June 8, Levine and Chamberlin met with the president of Germany, Paul von Hindenburg. In a rare honor, he presented the fliers with autographed photographs of himself. The welcomes, official and informal, continued. They were dinner guests at city hall, honored visitors to factories, and esteemed theater guests at the Civic Opera. A Berlin street was renamed *Columbia-Strasse*, and restaurants invented new dishes in tribute. One daring Berlin restaurant even offered Roast Beef a la Chamberlin, with Cottbus potatoes. At Tempelhof Airfield, Chamberlin noticed that *Cottbus* had been lightly scrawled on the side of the plane where the word *Paris* had been whited out in New York. Impressed, Chamberlin made the sentiment official. The words *New York–Berlin* now appeared on the plane with *Cottbus* beneath in smaller letters.

Chamberlin in Berlin

Clarence Chamberlin is hoisted above the crowd after landing the *Columbia* at Tempelhof Airfield in Berlin.

Dozens of business offers, some legitimate, arrived for the fliers at the embassy. Enterprising beer companies eagerly approached Chamberlin about naming a beer after him. Chamberlin was amused. He told a reporter, "When over here, I just sip enough wine to be polite in drinking toasts, and when I take a glass of beer I stand on that. I don't want more. It makes me sleepy. ..." Levine, ever on the lookout for new opportunities, floated his own ideas about forming companies to build and fly multiengined passenger planes across the Atlantic.

In the days that followed, the wining and dining continued without letup. No one was more appreciative of the lavish welcomes and meals than Chamberlin. The cash in his pocket added up to $11.14! Reporters, European and American, covered every move. One reporter asked Chamberlin, "Will you fly back?" The pilot smiled and answered, "Yes, on a boat!" Levine was a nonstop talker. He

Charles A. Levine (right) with Hearst newspaper reporter Cholly Knickerbocker in Berlin

Newspaper headline announcing the successful flight of Chamberlin and Levine aboard the *Columbia*

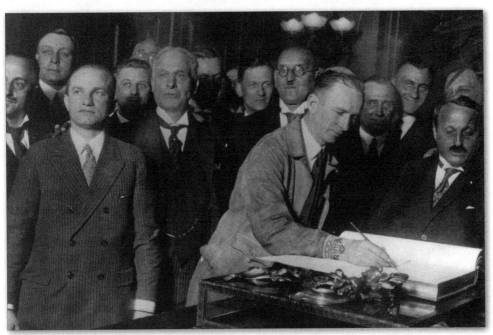

Chamberlin signing Visitors Book in Berlin

gave reporters—and anyone who would listen—conflicting information about his future plans. First, he announced that he would fly the *Columbia* back to America. Then he said he would tour Europe with the plane. He also said he was ready to invest millions of dollars to found a transatlantic airline.

As a dinner in their honor proceeded at the American Embassy, crowds outside chanted a traditional German cheer, *"Eins, zwei, [drei], Chamberlin! Eins, zwei, [drei], Levine!"* (One, two, three, Chamberlin! One, two, three, Levine!) In a sign of things to come in Germany, anti-Semitic newspapers refused to mention Levine's name in their articles about the flight of the *Columbia* and downplayed the lavish welcome of the two pilots.

On June 10, the two Americans laid a wreath at the tomb of Germany's famed World War I combat pilot Manfred von Richthofen, received a medal from the city of Berlin, and attended a dance that evening given in their honor by the American Club. They accepted an invitation to fly into neighboring countries. Austria was first. Just as Lindbergh had made courtesy flights into Belgium and Great Britain—America's wartime allies—Levine and Chamberlin concentrated on Germany's former partner during the Great War.

Meanwhile, across the ocean, Americans prepared to welcome Lindbergh home. Newspapers didn't know which side of the Atlantic to cover first. Front-page stories detailed Levine and Chamberlin's continuing adventures in Germany and, at the same time, described the feverish plans for Lindbergh's homecoming.

As Levine and Chamberlin continued with their ongoing social responsibilities, their wives were on a luxury steamship heading to Germany and a reunion with their husbands. Their midnight sailing from New York on the liner *Berlin* was a media event. Reporters mingled with six thousand well-wishers as camera flashes illuminated the night. When asked if she forgave her husband for sneaking off, Grace Levine graciously answered, "Of course, I'll forgive him ... I'm simply thrilled ... I'm most happy that I'm going to see my wonderful husband again." Mrs. Chamberlin repeated the sentiment. "I'm simply thrilled," she said.

The women had been feted at a celebration held by the Brooklyn Chamber of Commerce. Mrs. Chamberlin was presented with a check for her husband in the amount of $15,000. Mrs. Levine was given a diamond watch. Ralph Jonas, president of the chamber, spoke about the Brooklyn connections to the historic flight. When he spoke of the *Columbia*'s owner, he added, "Levine's ways were mysterious but ways of greatness."

While their wives made the leisurely trip across the Atlantic, Levine and Chamberlin flew to a health spa at Baden-Baden for rest and relaxation. Lufthansa put a plane at the men's disposal during their stay in Germany. Days later, on their way to greet their wives at the German port of Bremerhaven, they were feted by excited crowds of well-wishers at every stop. At the port, both men were taken out to sea in a motor boat and allowed to board the *Berlin* during the night. The wives were pleasantly surprised. When the ship docked, the reunited couples walked down the gangplank to waiting reporters and cheering admirers.

Again, Mrs. Levine was asked if she forgave her husband. "You bet," she said. "I think he is just wonderful!" Then the women joined their husbands in their hectic tour of German cities. Against their own initial wishes, the wives even agreed to fly. Charles Levine's freewheeling style was not in the least hindered by his wife's presence. When Germany's leading woman pilot, Thea Rasche, invited Levine to fly with her to demonstrate her skills with aeronautic acrobatics and daring loops, Mrs. Levine looked on disapprovingly. She told travel companions she "meant to have a serious talk with Charles." Levine's only comment about Rasche after returning to earth was, "She's some trick flyer ..."

The Americans returned to Berlin for a short but luxurious rest at the Hotel Adlon. The hundreds of gifts, big and small, lavished on the pilots were packed for shipment back to the United States. The pilots, their wives, and the reporters who accompanied them set off in three planes to continue the tour. Levine and Chamberlin flew the *Columbia* while the others traveled in two Lufthansa planes that followed. After a tumultuous reception in Munich, the party flew on to equally boisterous welcomes in Vienna, Austria, and, on June 22, in Budapest, Hungary.

Welcome to France

Levine and Chamberlin are surrounded by well-wishers upon their arrival at Le Bourget Airfield in Paris from Switzerland.

The honors, diplomatic receptions, and factory tours continued in Czechoslovakia. Occasionally, the rehearsed standard diplomatic etiquette was broken by an unexpected gesture. As the party entered a Marienbad, Czechoslovakia, restaurant, a young girl bearing a flower wreath rushed up and handed it to Mrs. Chamberlin.

While the wives boarded a train for Switzerland, Levine and Chamberlin flew on to Warsaw, Poland. After the usual round of welcomes there, they flew to Switzerland on June 29 to rejoin their wives. Flying through Europe provided Chamberlin with constant challenges. Fog, mist, and "blind flying" competed with unmapped routes and soaring mountains for the fliers' attention.

Levine and Chamberlin

The two pilots are carried off the field after the landing in Paris.

As the travelers prepared to go from Switzerland to Paris, news reached them that back at Roosevelt Field, Commander Byrd and his crew had finally taken off. At that very moment, the *America* was in the air, headed to France.

7

CLOSE ENOUGH

*"Can you visualize not being able to see the land or
the sea for over eighteen hours ..."*—Richard E. Byrd

For months, Commander Richard Byrd subjected his plane, *America*, to the most intense testing program aviation had ever seen. Byrd was on a self-imposed mission to prove to a skeptical public that transatlantic passenger aviation was not only possible but safe. "We wanted to show that some pay load could be carried across the Atlantic," Byrd explained. The test flights, weight-

The *America* in front of its hangar

load calculations, takeoff field preparations, and instrument calibrations took time and money to complete. Money was not a problem. The entire flight program was underwritten by wealthy businessman Rodman Wanamaker. As improvements were made to Roosevelt Field, Byrd "personally went over every inch of the ground." A crew of four was scheduled to be onboard "to demonstrate that passengers could even now be taken across the Atlantic."

The plane Byrd selected was a specially modified version of a Fokker C-2.

The famous explorer

Commander Richard E. Byrd was a famed Arctic explorer. Before flying the *America* across the Atlantic in 1927, Byrd had already flown to the North Pole. After his transatlantic flight, he led an expedition to Antarctica. Above, he is shown in front of the plane he flew to the frozen continent, and on the right he is shown in his cold-weather gear.

Byrd had used a Fokker plane during his Arctic expedition and was familiar with the designer and his work. It was a big plane for its time, powered by three Wright J-5 Whirlwind engines, the same engine that powered the *Spirit of St. Louis* and the *Columbia*. Byrd, unlike Lindbergh, believed in the reliability of a multiengined plane for transatlantic flight. "If anything went wrong with a single engine," Byrd reasoned, "the expedition would end then and there, and the prestige of aviation ... would be damaged in the public mind." The plane's wing, built in Holland, was seventy-one feet in length. The fuel tanks held a total of 1,295 gallons, more than enough for a transatlantic flight.

The *America* was christened at Roosevelt Field on May 25, just a few days after news of Lindbergh's safe arrival in Paris reached New York. Over the

The *America*

The *America* sits at Roosevelt Field just prior to its christening ceremony.

following weeks, a number of takeoffs were scheduled, each postponed for varying reasons. Byrd first waited for the Lindbergh receptions and parades to end so as not to detract from the young flier's momentous accomplishment. On June 13, Lindbergh's triumphant ticker-tape parade took place in New York. That same day, Byrd publicly announced that the *America*'s destination would be Paris. He then waited for the weather over the Atlantic to clear. "If I were on my own," he told a reporter, "I probably would take off. But I've got three men with me. ... If we should fail by disregarding weather advices it might do a serious injury to aviation."

Some observers began to doubt Byrd's resolve. After the successful flights of Lindbergh and Levine and Chamberlin, Byrd began receiving letters blaming him for purposely delaying takeoff of the *America*. Some went so far as to accuse the legendary polar explorer of cowardice. Even Fokker, the plane's designer, was disillusioned. He told a reporter that the work at Roosevelt Field was "the most interminable series of test flights it has ever been my grief to witness." The criticism did not alter Byrd's behavior. "I admit," he later wrote, "it would have been gratifying to be first across; but that was only a secondary consideration. ... We were in no race."

As everyone waited for the weather to clear, Byrd found time to travel to Yale University in New Haven, Connecticut, to receive an honorary degree. On June 25, 1927, the words *Peace* and *Airmail* were prominently painted on the *America* to highlight the flight's scientific purpose and the swearing-in of Commander Byrd as the first official United States transatlantic airmail pilot. As curious crowds continued to gather daily at Roosevelt Field, an exasperated Fokker shrugged and told anyone who would listen, "Well, she's ready. What more can I do?"

Mechanics and experts continued their tinkering, although the *America* seemed prepared for every possible problem that could arise. It was the first plane equipped with a "dump valve" to "empty our fuel in a few seconds in case we saw we were going to crash." Catwalks were installed so one of the fliers could reach the engine during flight if a malfunction arose. A special switch was added to cut off all three engines at once in the event of a fire. Thermometers were fastened around the outside of the plane so the crew could detect icing problems. The instrument panels in the cockpit were luminous so they could be read if the lights onboard failed. A "putty-like substance" was stored on the plane to fix any leaks in the huge gas tank. Two fuel lines were run to each engine in case one line clogged.

The plane was also equipped with the latest technological instruments. A wind-drift indicator would alert the crew if the plane were off course. A sextant, specially designed by Byrd himself, could show their exact position in midflight. Most important to Byrd was the radio. Lindbergh and Chamberlin, concerned about any extra weight on their smaller planes, eliminated the heavy radio equipment from their aircraft. Although radio broadcast range was limited, it would allow the crew to contact ships in midocean. An automatic signal would also broadcast the plane's position.

Improvements to the runway did not guarantee that the field was long enough for the large, loaded plane to gather enough speed for a takeoff. To solve that problem, a unique sixty-foot wooden inclined ramp was built. The idea was simple. Place the *America* on the ramp. Hold it back with a strong rope while the engines warm up to maximum speed. Then cut the rope, allowing the plane to propel down the ramp and onto the runway with enough speed for a successful takeoff. It was a novel idea.

All the engineering skills and technological devices could not overcome the continuous bad weather that plagued the flight's takeoff. Doc Kimball of the United States Weather Bureau, who had provided important help to both the *Spirit of St. Louis* and the *Columbia*, turned his professional attention to the *America*. In an age before weather satellites and radar, he relied on radioed weather reports from ships at sea to plot weather conditions over the Atlantic.

As the rain and fog remained, ground crews continued to make the *America* ready. Each day, crowds of onlookers arrived, hoping to witness the historic takeoff. Each day, they went home disappointed. Finally, in the early morning hours of June 29, Doc Kimball notified Byrd that an opportunity existed for flight. At Roosevelt Field, rain was still falling. But Kimball's radio reports indicated that weather over the Atlantic, although not perfect, was clearing up.

At the nearby Garden City Hotel, the crew was awakened at 3:00 a.m. Byrd had selected three expert fliers to accompany him. Bernt Balchen had advised Byrd on his North Pole flight. Bert Acosta was an experienced pilot, a former barnstormer. Lieutenant George Noville was the radio operator. As the men gathered at Roosevelt Field, final adjustments were made on the plane, and the last gallons of fuel were filtered by hand into the tank. Last-minute supplies were loaded aboard. Food for the crew included four roast chickens, sixteen chicken sandwiches, sixteen ham-and-cheese sandwiches, coffee, and tea. As the rain continued, a post office truck delivered a bag of mail to be carried to Paris.

During the night, word had spread to reporters, and a growing crowd gathered in the rain and darkness to witness the takeoff. Byrd later recalled, "When I reached the field at 3.00 A.M., June 29th, the plane was at the top of our little hill and, by the aid of powerful lights, the crew was applying the finishing touches." Harold "Doc" Kinkaid of the Wright Aeronautical Company, who had overseen the J-5 engines on the *Spirit of St Louis* and the *Columbia*, tinkered with *America*'s J-5 engines and reported to Byrd, "They're as good as they can be, Commander." "I know they are, Doc," Byrd responded.

The crew said their good-byes to relatives and friends and climbed aboard the *America*. Bert Acosta sat in the pilot's seat; next to him was Bernt Balchen. George Noville hunched behind them with his hand poised on the fuel-dump valve. In the event of an impending crash, his job was to empty the fuel tank to prevent an inferno. Byrd, who was acting as the flight's navigator, stood behind Balchen during takeoff. Outside, behind the plane stood a mechanic with an ax ready to cut the rope once the plane's engines were fully revved up, thereby releasing the plane down the incline. He never got the chance to perform his assigned task.

Before the engines reached full power, the rope snapped and the plane began a premature slide down the incline. The time was 5:24 a.m. Acosta was faced with a split-second decision to either cut the engines and stop the flight or

The *America*

The Fokker aircraft *America* rests on the inclined platform prior to takeoff.

continue. He decided to continue but kept an arm raised, ready to signal Noville to instantly activate the dump valve. The plane accelerated down the runway. Roosevelt Field was 5,000 feet long with a row of hangars at the very end. To onlookers, it seemed as if the huge plane, weighing over 17,000 pounds, would never become airborne before smashing into the hangars. Finally, forty-eight agonizing seconds later, the plane lifted off the ground after rolling 3,270 feet down the runway at 80 miles per hour. People on the ground held their breaths as the *America* finally gained altitude to clear the hangars. They were aloft! Acosta turned to Balchen with a smile. "Whatta helluva take-off that was!" he said.

Despite all the detailed planning and testing, their exciting takeoff was only an indication of a harrowing flight to come. Early radio messages to the ground crew from the plane provided no indication of problems. 6:00 a.m.: "Everything going fine. Noville." 7:22: "Passed Cape Cod, two miles west of Cape Cod Light. All well. Byrd." 8:10: "Weather clearing en route Cape Cod to Yarmouth. Out of sight of land. Extra cans of gas causing trouble with compasses. Byrd." 1:30 p.m.: "We are keeping sharp lookout for Nungesser and Coli ... flying at 5000 feet." 5:12 p.m.: "Crew in good condition. Head winds are bothering us. Cape Race is the last station we will raise on the coast. Regards to hangar crew. Byrd."

By the time the *America* reached Newfoundland, weather and visibility worsened. Rain and dense fog totally enveloped the plane. The crew was flying blind, depending on their instruments for crucial information. At 6:39 p.m., Byrd sent the following message: "Dense fog covers all Newfoundland. Have had adverse winds. Impossible to navigate. Can hardly see wingtips." Those conditions would not change for the rest of their flight. Byrd later remarked, "I hope no other pilots have that experience. It is not a very pleasant one."

At one point, Balchen handed controls over to Acosta. Almost immediately, Balchen felt the plane go into a dangerous spiral toward the ground. He quickly grabbed control of the plane back from Acosta and, through skillful maneuvering, finally righted the plane and averted disaster. Acosta made an embarrassing admission. "This instrument flying is one thing I've never bothered with," he told his astonished colleagues.

The crew was feeling colder. Byrd, alert for icing, kept an eye on the thermometers attached to the wing struts. When they were still over Newfoundland, Noville handed a disturbing note to Byrd. According to Noville's calculations, they were burning more fuel than anticipated. If they continued to fight winds and bad weather, there would not be enough fuel to reach Paris. Byrd kept the information to himself. He did not want to alarm the others. "If I were wrong," Byrd later said, "then we should fall into the sea and be lost before making a landfall on the other side."

After twenty-four hours in the air, Byrd sent another dispiriting message. "We have seen neither land or sea since 3 o'clock yesterday. Everything completely covered with fog. Whatever happens I take my hat off to these great fellows."

On and on they flew into the inky darkness. Occasionally, the fliers' spirits were lifted by radio messages from ships far below them. Otherwise, they were alone, unable to see out their windows and unsure of their course. Byrd made the following notations in his log. "It is impossible to navigate. Ice is forming on the plane." Occasionally, they were able to fly above the clouds. "It was a weird sight," Byrd later said, "to look down from the pinnacle of black masses we were skimming. ... The fire from the exhaust pipes of our faithful engines, invisible in the daytime, shone vividly in the dark night."

As they flew on, Noville made a dramatic—and happy—discovery about the *America*'s fuel. "I made a mistake in the first estimate," he notified Byrd. "We have enough gasoline left to fly to Rome." A relieved Byrd replied, "Wish I had known that 18 hours ago."

On the afternoon of their second day aloft, the *America* broke out of the blind fog. Below, the fliers could see the rough ocean. The number of radio messages from land increased, indicating they were close to Europe. Their joy was short-lived as radio reports indicated that their destination, Paris, was also enveloped in thick fog. Byrd, however, radioed an optimistic message: "Hope to sight land within an hour. Crew fine after a strenuous trip." Onboard the *America*, the crew kept a lookout for land. Then, through the clouds, at 5:00 p.m. local time, they spotted Brest, France. They were nearly two hundred miles off their intended course. Byrd ordered his crew to continue flying along the coast of France and then follow the course of the Seine River directly into Paris. Although that course added two hours to the flight, Byrd reasoned that was the safest way of approaching the fogged-in city. As they continued toward Paris in the wind and rain, the darkness of the approaching night and the rolling fog dropped visibility to near zero.

According to Commander Byrd's calculations, they should be arriving at Le Bourget Airfield, northeast of Paris, at 10:00 p.m. As the hour approached, the crew strained to catch sight of the airport beacon. "I am flying around Paris," Byrd radioed. "Don't know whether we'll land Paris or elsewhere. Give me my position." A cheerful crowd estimated at more than twenty thousand waited expectantly at the airport. Among them were Levine and Chamberlin. Earlier in the day, the two fliers had flown into Le Bourget from Berne, Switzerland, in time to dedicate a plaque at the airport in honor of Lindbergh's successful flight. Two revolving searchlights illuminated the sky. Periodically, airport staff fired rockets into the air. Rain and wind constantly whipped over the runway. The crew aboard the *America* saw nothing as they continued flying through the thick fog. They were lost.

When told of Byrd's expected arrival, Chamberlin told a reporter, "That makes three who have done it—never two without three!" But when it became clear the *America* would not land as scheduled, Levine and Chamberlin arranged to protect the *Columbia* with a police guard and went to Paris to await further news at their hotel. "They will never be able to find the airdrome in this," Levine said.

At 12:44 a.m., Byrd sent the first of several emergency SOS radio signals. "Lost. Only three hours of gas left." There was little anyone on the ground could do. The terrible weather conditions prevented search planes from taking off. From time to time, the huge throng grew silent as people strained in vain to listen for the plane. All they could do was wait. Across the Atlantic in a hangar at Roosevelt Field, reporters and friends stood by nervously for news of the flight. To the stirring music of a band, those present burst into shouts of joy when they were told, incorrectly, that the *America* had been sighted over Paris. "They're there! They're there!" shouted Mrs. Acosta. Celebratory rockets were shot into the air in New York.

Over France, meanwhile, at 3:00 a.m., the last SOS was received from the *America*: "Lost in the wind and the rain."

Suddenly, through a break in the fog, Byrd caught sight of a lighthouse's revolving light. "I knew there was no ocean lighthouse near Paris," he later said. "We were somewhere on the coast of France! I was astonished very greatly indeed. The compass had gone wrong—had taken us in a great circle." After making a few adjustments, they headed back through the wind, rain, and darkness toward Paris. Their fuel was nearly exhausted. Byrd realized there was no chance the aircraft could land at Le Bourget, even if he could find it. With no indication the plane could come down safely on land, he ordered the *America* turned back toward the lighthouse and the ocean. "There was nothing else we could do under the circumstances," Byrd later explained, "that would give us any chance whatever to save the lives of the crew and to avoid endangering the people beneath us."

Bernt Balchen was in the pilot's seat; next to him sat Acosta. Byrd and Noville braced themselves in the rear. As the plane descended, they caught sight of an electric sign on the roof of a building below them. *Deauville* alerted them they were south of Le Havre on the coast of Normandy and two and a half hours from Paris. Soon, the lighthouse came into view. There was a beach close by, but it appeared to be too rocky to use as a runway. "Stand by to land," Byrd alerted his crew. The *America* would have to come down in the ocean. "There's a danger of capsizing if we do that," said Noville. "I know," Byrd answered, "but is there any alternative?"

They dropped three flares into the water to illuminate the landing site as the plane continued its descent. Byrd and Noville ripped out the two side windows as escape routes and braced themselves. Balchen decreased the plane's speed, and the wheels skimmed the water, shearing off the landing gear. Noville's head sharply hit the fuselage, knocking him briefly unconscious. Forty-three hours and twenty-one minutes after taking off from Roosevelt Field, the *America* came to a violent stop with its tail in the air, two hundred yards offshore from the village of Ver-sur-Mer. It came to rest in the water in view of the lighthouse that had guided them to safety. Balchen later modestly said, "I am glad things ended as well as they did. They could have ended worse."

Commander Byrd was thrown out of one window while Noville climbed out the one on the other side. "Dick, where are you?" he yelled into the darkness. Acosta had been thrown through the front window, fracturing his collarbone. After a few moments, Byrd and Noville climbed aboard the wings, which were only partially submerged. With alarm they realized that Bernt Balchen was

The *America* in the water

After a troubled flight over the Atlantic, Commander Byrd
ordered the plane down in the ocean off the coast of France
because heavy fog and depleted fuel would not permit
a landing in Paris.

missing. Instantly, Byrd dove into the water. Within minutes Balchen was sighted
swimming in the water and was helped aboard the wing. Byrd made one other
dive into the submerged fuselage of the plane to retrieve a lockbox that contained
a priceless piece of flag sewn by Betsy Ross, which was to be presented as a gift
to the president of France.

Somehow they managed to inflate a rubber raft and help each other aboard.
"We were stiff and bruised, tired and watersoaked," Byrd recalled. Noville had
gone back into the plane to rescue the official U.S. Post Office Department
mailbag entrusted to their care. They placed the lockbox bearing the piece of
flag and the mailbag in a dry compartment in the wing. Then, glad to be alive,

they paddled toward the welcoming beacon of the lighthouse.

That light was the only welcome the brave fliers received. Not a soul was in sight except for a boy on a bicycle who, taking one look at the unshaven, drenched men from the sea, hastily pedaled away. They headed toward the little village of Ver-sur-Mer and went door-to-door trying to rouse people from their beds, but to no avail. Finally, they reached the lighthouse, where the keeper and his wife, after realizing that the grubby strangers before them had really flown from the United States, graciously offered food, hot drink, and warm clothes. Slowly, other townspeople gathered in great excitement and good cheer. Amid the festivities, the pilots continued to think about their plane.

The tide was going out and the *America*, submerged for only a short time, now sat dry and easily accessible. While Acosta and Noville remained behind with their new friends, Byrd and Balchen headed back to the plane to retrieve the mail, flag piece, and whatever records they could salvage. Townspeople followed them and helped carry items from the plane to shore. The exhausted fliers then went to sleep in village houses as honored guests. While they slept soundly for thirteen hours, the world was informed of their amazing ordeal and safety. Sailors from a local naval base arrived to dismantle the *America* and transport it to the nearby port of Cherbourg for eventual shipment back to the United States.

Byrd cabled Rodman Wanamaker, "Deeply sorry we didn't reach Paris." Wanamaker gallantly responded, "We are all overwhelmed with joy. ... The greatest air battle of the world has been fought."

Later, when recounting the historic trip, Byrd wrote, "So long as we live we can never forget the kindness of the people of Ver-sur-Mer, and before leaving France we motored back there to tell them 'good-bye.'"

8

GLORY!

"Levine's ways were mysterious, but ways of greatness."
—Ralph Jonas, Brooklyn Chamber of Commerce

Byrd's reception by the French was no less enthusiastic than the welcome shown Charles A. Lindbergh just weeks earlier. Across the ocean on that Friday, July 1, 1927, the *New York Times* issued an extra edition at 4:30 a.m. to announce Byrd's heart-stopping arrival. When told about Byrd's successful but plagued flight, Lindbergh responded, "That's too bad. I am sorry it happened that way. Byrd and his crew are wonderful men and aviators!"

Wreckage of the *America*

The big plane sank to the wings in the water off Ver-sur-Mer, France, after it landed.

On the evening of their unceremonious arrival in France, the exhausted crew of the *America* seemed quiet and subdued at a hastily arranged banquet in their honor in Caen, a nearby city. As they ate and drank, the reality of their nearly fatal ordeal sunk in. The next morning, after a few hours of refreshing sleep, they stepped onto a train for the journey to Paris. At the Gare Saint Lazare train station in Paris, an exuberant crowd of twenty-five thousand people blocked traffic in surrounding streets to cheer their heroes. Among them were Levine and Chamberlin. After a motorcade to the Hotel Continental and a short rest, the crew was received by French president Gaston Doumergue. Byrd presented the president with the piece of Betsy Ross's flag, and in return, the president made the American commander an Officer of the French Legion of Honor.

The men received cables of congratulations from American dignitaries,

Honoring Lindbergh

Upon landing in Paris, Levine and Chamberlin were invited to participate in a special ceremony dedicating a plaque at Le Bourget Airfield to honor Charles A. Lindbergh.

Ticket to a reception

This ticket of admission permitted entrance to the official reception for Levine, Chamberlin, and Byrd and his crew held by the city of Paris on July 7, 1927.

including President Calvin Coolidge. The secretary of the Navy wrote, "Well done, Byrd!" Later, at the Paris City Hall, before an enthusiastic crowd of thirty-five thousand Parisians, Byrd and his crew members were each presented with gold medals. Just as Lindbergh, Chamberlin, and Levine had been previously acclaimed, it was now the turn of Byrd and the *America*'s crew to be wined, dined, and honored. They were guests at a Fourth of July banquet, a luncheon given by the English-American Press Club, and a reception by the Aero Club of France. Byrd laid a wreath at the Tomb of the Unknown Soldier at the Arc de Triomphe. He also paid a solemn visit, as Lindbergh had done, to Nungesser's mother. At some events, they were joined by Levine and Chamberlin, who were totally at home amid all the fame.

From the moment Levine landed in Europe, he had been confounding everyone with schemes and plans that made headlines throughout Europe and the United States. When he announced that he was planning to fly back to America on the *Columbia*, even Chamberlin was amazed. "I knew only too well what a hazardous thing a trans-Atlantic flight in a single-motored plane is, and did not care to ride my luck too hard by attempting to fly back." He and his wife prepared to sail back to the United States with Commander Byrd and the *America*'s crew.

All the while, Charles A. Levine remained comfortably in Europe. On July 7, Levine made another announcement. He would indeed fly the *Columbia* back to New York but with a new pilot, French World War I air hero Maurice Drouhin. To Levine's surprise, the French were not overjoyed. Drouhin had been working on flying a French-built plane across the Atlantic. French pride was hurt because he now planned to fly an American plane.

The next day, Levine, Chamberlin, and Drouhin flew the *Columbia* from Paris to London to familiarize the new pilot with the plane. Mrs. Chamberlin followed behind as a passenger in another airplane. From the beginning, problems arose that threatened the new relationship between Levine and Drouhin. First, Drouhin knew no English; Levine, no French. Recognizing the importance of being able to communicate during a dangerous transatlantic flight, Levine began taking French lessons when he returned to Paris. Second, mistrust developed between them. Despite a written contract, Drouhin began to suspect that the *Columbia*'s owner might replace him with another pilot. Levine began to think that Drouhin might try to take off without him. Their wariness of each other increased. Levine went so far as to remove a part of the engine to prevent the plane from taking off. "Apparently," Drouhin wryly commented, "Mr. Levine has no confidence in me."

Meanwhile, Clarence Chamberlin boarded the *Leviathan* in Southampton, England, where Levine bid him a bon voyage. Byrd and his crew joined the ship when it docked in Cherbourg, France. Before leaving, the crew of the *America* returned to the little coastal village of Ver-sur-Mer for an emotional farewell with the people who had opened their hearts and doors to the fliers just days earlier. Byrd wanted to see once more the room he had slept in. He was amazed!

It was precisely as he had left it—as a "shrine"—with left-behind mementos, including a pack of cigarettes and some chewing gum. A crowd of townspeople gathered in front of the modest house. When Byrd emerged, mothers thrust their little babies at him. To the delight of everyone, he obliged by kissing them all.

For the aviators, the ocean voyage offered a welcome rest from the hustle and bustle surrounding their achievements. The days were relaxed and informal and the evenings filled with formal dinners and receptions. Chamberlin later said, "I really didn't appreciate how much water I had flown over until I returned on the *Leviathan*." Their restful voyage home would soon end with the most tumultuous harbor welcome New York had ever seen.

When the *Leviathan* reached New York on that rainy July 18, everything was ready for another ticker-tape welcome. At the entrance to New York Harbor, the fliers left their liner and boarded the *Macom*, the official city yacht, for the trip through the bay to Battery Park on the tip of Manhattan. Awaiting them

Tons of paper

First Lindbergh, then Byrd and Chamberlin were celebrated in huge ticker-tape parades in New York (above) and other American cities.

were family members, eager to embrace their heroes. Along the route to shore, a convoy of ships of all sizes accompanied them as the ships' horns and sirens joyfully announced the aviators' safe return. Mrs. Byrd could only smile happily at her husband: her words were drowned out by the noise. Fireboats saluted with streams of water as, overhead, airplanes continuously circled the convoy.

Onboard the *Macom* was Charles A. Lindbergh. Chamberlin later recalled that Lindy came to greet his colleagues "with real sincerity and no ostentation." When photographers assembled the five aviators on the *Macom*'s rear deck for group shots, they called, "Lindy! Lindy! Lindy!" But Lindbergh stayed on the sidelines and out of the photographs. When the *Macom* landed its world-famous passengers, Lindbergh quietly slipped away. "I had my day," he said.

Byrd, Acosta, Noville, Balchen, and Chamberlin were escorted to their waiting open cars for the triumphant rain-soaked parade up Broadway, where millions of cheering New Yorkers awaited under umbrellas. Byrd, dressed in his white naval officer's uniform, simply told his welcomers, "Good to be back." When asked what he thought about his flight, Byrd responded that the trip demonstrated that airplanes could travel in any weather. This was Byrd's second ticker-tape parade in two years; the first, on June 23, 1926, honored his adventurous flight to the North Pole. American flags hung from the many towering office buildings. In honor of Chamberlin's flight, a German flag appeared out of the window of the German consulate.

The parade's progress was broadcast live over a National Broadcasting Company hookup of sixteen radio stations. For millions of Americans sitting comfortably—and dry—at home, it was almost as exciting as being on Broadway. The four announcers stationed along the parade route conveyed the feeling of excitement displayed by people on the street. "The windows are jammed with people," radio announcer Graham McNamee told listeners, "the parade has started, and its front end is just turning northward at the corner of Bowling Green." Even the damp crowds on lower Broadway benefited from new technology when huge loudspeakers, recently invented by the Westinghouse Electric Company, boomed the radio announcers' words for a distance of six blocks.

Welcome home

The ticker-tape parade in New York for Chamberlin, Byrd, and the crew of the *America* brought out thousands despite on-and-off showers.

At City Hall, Mayor James J. Walker presented the five aviators with New York City's Medal of Honor. "This seems to be my weather," Byrd said. "It rained when we started, it rained when we reached France, and now look at what it's done!" He also told the cheering crowd, "I think you are heroes to stay here in the rain to hear me."

Celebrations continued for the returned aviators. The fliers and their families were feted at receptions and dinners. Only Bernt Balchen, a bachelor with no family in New York, seemed uncomfortable at these gala events. At a formal dinner on July 19, broadcast live over radio, speakers extolled the bravery of the men. The secretary of the Navy, Curtis Wilbur, representing President Coolidge, presented Commander Richard E. Byrd and Lieutenant George Noville with Distinguished Flying Cross medals. (The remaining crew members were not eligible for the award: Acosta was not a military officer and Balchen was not a United States citizen.) To the assembled crowd, Byrd delivered a speech on his

Byrd triumphant

Commander Richard E. Byrd was honored in an emotional homecoming parade in Boston.

exploits and the future of aviation. "Can you visualize not being able to see the land or the sea for over eighteen hours ...," he asked the stilled crowd. Then, speaking of his crew, he added, "[D]uring all that time those fellows kept on and obeyed orders and functioned perfectly as an organization."

Chamberlin spoke next. "We had a little more good fortune than Commander Byrd and his party," he said. "We had our share of fog, but we were able to finish in daylight and see what we were doing." Then, in a noble gesture to his flying partner who was not present, Chamberlin added, "No one knew Mr. Levine was going until they saw me open the throttle and take him with me. Naturally, most people, not knowing anything of his flying ability, thought he was merely a passenger. While he is not a professional pilot, he was of great assistance ... without not only his services but his financing it would not have been possible for me."

Meanwhile, back in Europe Levine continued to generate even more publicity with new business proposals, including one $10 million scheme to operate a transatlantic air cargo and mail service. Rumors surfaced about a race between the *Columbia* and a French airplane and crew from Paris to New York. Newspapers reported on preparations to get the *Columbia* ready and on Levine's continuing French lessons. Mrs. Levine, one newspaper reported, was in charge of preparing the food for the flight.

Behind the scenes, Drouhin, the French pilot, was still unhappy. Levine refused to provide money for Mrs. Drouhin in the event of the pilot's death during the flight. Likewise, a rumor surfaced that Levine was actually negotiating with an English pilot to replace Drouhin. Although Levine denied this with a public statement in support of Drouhin, the French pilot was quickly losing faith in his American partner. Drouhin then threatened to fly to New York on the *Columbia* with another French pilot and stationed his friends to guard the plane. As a further step, a French court issued an injunction prohibiting anyone but Drouhin to fly the *Columbia* in accordance with his contract with Levine.

Not to be outwitted, Levine went to Le Bourget Airfield on August 29 and told a policeman guarding the plane that he wanted to warm up the engine and taxi the *Columbia* up and down the runway. There seemed nothing wrong with that, and the policeman and a mechanic helped Levine move the plane out of the hangar. To the astonishment of people at the airport, Levine applied power to the engine, taxied to the end of the runway, and took off. Two of Drouhin's friends started for a nearby plane to give pursuit but quickly gave up. The Bellanca was faster than any plane on the field. News was quickly radioed across the English Channel. Levine was heading toward London. Mrs. Levine, in her hotel room, was stunned when she heard the news. Her husband had never before flown an airplane by himself.

At Croydon Airfield in London, preparations were hurriedly made to receive the intrepid traveler, "a flying man who couldn't fly!" At 4:30 that afternoon, watchers at the airport sighted the *Columbia*. Sirens blared and all air traffic in the area was suspended for Levine's landing. Fire engines and an ambulance stood by. Pilots on the ground were struck with horror. It was clear that Levine really didn't know how to land. He was close to stalling the plane, which would result in a disastrous crash. On his first pass over the airport, he flew in too fast, turned, and climbed to position himself for another attempt. One pilot, sensing the danger, climbed into a waiting plane, went aloft, and safely guided Levine down using hand signals. Levine later recalled, "I didn't see the ambulance, but I saw the fire trucks. I hoped they wouldn't have to use them. I thought I was getting along fairly well until I saw all the excitement down below. Then I began to think perhaps I wasn't so good as I thought I was."

Describing Mr. Levine's unorthodox arrival, the *London Times* commented, "The arrival and subsequent landing by Mr. Levine on Croydon Aerodrome was the most alarming experience which has happened in the memory of civil aviation traffic officers, regular pilots and aerodrome staff."

As unfriendly airport officials approached the *Columbia*, Levine emerged with a grin and said, "Hello. I think I need a shave, I didn't know I was coming." In response, one officer quipped, "You've already had a close shave." Aside from

Charles A. Levine with British pilot Walter Hinchliffe

Levine, still dressed in his white flight suit, is photographed shortly after making his heart-stopping landing at Croydon Airfield.

the angry airport welcome, the rest of England was delighted with Levine's daring flight. They were even happier when Levine announced he was replacing Drouhin with British pilot Walter Hinchliffe. That evening, when Levine went to the theater, the audience greeted him warmly with applause.

"I'm fed up with the French," Levine undiplomatically said. "They've been getting at me from the start just because I didn't land in Paris first." Levine eventually paid Drouhin a small fee for canceling his contract. Grace Levine, tired of the endless European adventure, returned alone to the United States while her husband continued to plan for the transatlantic trip with the new pilot. In September, Levine finally announced that he was giving up on his plans to fly back to the United States because of the continuing bad weather. "I am no madcap," he told reporters. Then he and Hinchliffe set off on a trip to India but

Safely in England

Charles A. Levine (dressed in white) leads the *Columbia* into a hangar at Croydon Airfield after his near-disastrous flight from Paris. British police help push.

got only as far as Venice, Italy, because of a malfunctioning propeller.

From Venice, Levine went on to Rome, where he was received by Pope Pius XI, before whom the usually talkative Levine could only stammer a few words. He also visited the Italian dictator, Benito Mussolini. Levine regarded Mussolini as "the greatest man in the world." The feeling was mutual since the dictator considered himself a fan of the American. He thought Levine's solo crossing of the English Channel was a brave and noble act. Earlier, when the *Columbia* had originally landed in Germany, Mussolini sent a congratulatory telegram to the American ambassador in Germany expressing his "profound admiration ... for this second flight across the ocean which has been accomplished by Chamberlin and Levine in a plane designed and constructed by an Italian."

By October, it was time for Levine to return home. The United States government wanted to question him about some earlier business dealings. He did not fly back. Both Levine and the *Columbia* returned home by boat. When a reporter asked Mrs. Levine about her husband's return, she responded, "He is a hero in my eyes no matter what anyone else can say."

The welcome for Levine was less rousing than for Lindbergh, Byrd, and Chamberlin. Public interest had shifted to other newsworthy events. Nonetheless, Levine, who also sailed home on the *Leviathan*, was met by the *Macom* in New York Harbor. Onboard, among the dignitaries, were Grace Levine and one of their two daughters. A small motorcade, minus the ticker tape and large crowds, proceeded to the Biltmore Hotel, where Levine could rest awhile. There he received a congratulatory call from Clarence Chamberlin. Later, at City Hall, there was a short welcoming ceremony by the mayor and the presentation of a scroll of honor. Along the sparsely lined route to City Hall, one policeman shouted, "You came back too late!" Then he was off to an official luncheon with hundreds of guests at the Hotel Astor.

Alluding to negative rumors about Levine's business methods, and anti-Semitic comments that had begun to surface, Mayor Walker told Levine "how proud we are of you" and then added a bit of advice. "I can't tell you anything about flying, but from my experience I would make you a little suggestion. No matter what they say, if you feel right and know you are right, pay off all knocks with a smile."

New York congressman Hamilton Fish said, "The American people and the citizens of New York do not seem to appreciate Mr. Levine's accomplishment. He was not a passenger in the plane. He owned it and gambled it and his own life and won. They cannot take that glory away from him."

Levine responded, "Fate has been very kind to me. After four months of excitement, I am returned to the bosom of my family and friends, there to receive tributes as generous as they are undeserved."

9

FRONTIER OF FLIGHT

"New York to Paris—it sounds like a dream."
—Charles A. Lindbergh

Today, when huge jet airliners carry hundreds of people and tons of cargo around the globe, a flight from New York to Paris is not in the least unusual. Travelers from New York can fly to South Africa or Taiwan in less than a day. Before 1927, such flights seemed as impossible as a trip to Mars. The dramatic flights of the *Spirit of St. Louis*, the *Columbia*, and the *America* changed the world. The successes of Lindbergh, Chamberlin, Levine, Byrd, Balchen, Acosta, and Noville would not have been possible without the unsung contributions of others who shared their vision of aviation. Lindy may have been called the Lone Eagle, but his feat would not have succeeded without the dedication of others. It should not be forgotten that brave aviators—Davis, Wooster, Nungesser, Coli, Clavier, Islamoff, and others—died in unsuccessful attempts to fly across the Atlantic before Lindbergh. Charles L. Lawrance designed the Wright Whirlwind J-5 engine that powered each of the successful airplanes. His revolutionary air-cooled engine made the J-5 lighter than others of its power. Coupled with the ability to conserve fuel, the engine was extremely reliable for long-distance flights. Interestingly, when the Collier Trophy for the best annual contribution to aviation was presented for 1927, the award did not go to any of the headline-making pilots but to Mr. Lawrance for his magnificent engine.

Dr. James H. "Doc" Kimball of the United States Weather Bureau was the official weather consultant for each of the three flights. Next to the airplane's reliability, knowledge of weather conditions over the Atlantic Ocean was crucial.

Using innovative methods, including radio transmissions about weather conditions from ships at sea, Doc Kimball pieced together his best professional guess of the conditions the pilots could expect. His reaction to the nearly disastrous flight of the *America* was "forty-two invaluable hours. Nothing in meteorological history to compare to it!"

Donald Hall was the chief engineer for the Ryan Flying Company. When Lindbergh approached the company to build the *Spirit of St. Louis*, Hall understood that the lanky young pilot really needed a specially designed plane if he were to succeed. Hall and the employees of Ryan accepted the challenge to build the best airplane they could in the limited time available to them. Work proceeded day and night, with Lindbergh overseeing every detail of the plane's

Mr. & Mrs. Charles A. Lindbergh

Lindbergh and his wife, Anne Morrow Lindbergh, seen here in Paris, enjoyed travel. Anne Lindbergh was a pilot and a noted author.

construction. The result was a carefully crafted airplane designed to withstand the rigors of an uncharted Atlantic flight.

John Carisi was chief mechanic for Columbia Aviation. He supervised every aspect of the *Columbia*'s preparation for the record flight. When Levine planned to fly back from Europe, Carisi came over to supervise the installation of a new Whirlwind engine.

Harold "Doc" Kinkaid worked for the Wright Aeronautical Corporation. He was assigned to each of the three flights to fine-tune the Whirlwind engines. Indeed, the pilots would not take off without his approval. "Never heard a motor sound better," he reassured a mechanic before the *Columbia* took off.

Brice Goldsborough of Pioneer Instrument personally directed the installation and calibration of that company's new earth inductor compass system in each of the three planes. Although each plane had difficulty using it, the system was the forerunner of later aviation navigation systems that revolutionized air travel.

Lindbergh was the American hero of his generation. On a goodwill flight to Mexico City with the *Spirit of St. Louis*, he met, fell in love with, and soon married Anne Morrow, daughter of the American ambassador to Mexico. Their early years together were idyllic but far from quiet. As much as the Lindberghs yearned for a private life, they were constantly besieged by well-wishers. Any attempt at a normal life was shattered in March 1932 when Charles A. Lindbergh Jr., infant son of Charles and Anne, was kidnapped and killed. The "Crime of the Century" captured the interest of people around the world.

Lindbergh's hero status was tarnished in the minds of many by his isolationist, pro-German, and blatantly anti-Semitic views prior to World War II. He strongly believed that the United States should not become involved in foreign wars. Even when he volunteered his services and helped strengthen U.S. air power once the country was attacked by Japan, his reputation had been sharply damaged. Yet in 1954, his book *The Spirit of St. Louis*, which brilliantly recounted the 1927 flight, was awarded that year's Pulitzer Prize for literature. Ever curious to solve problems, he made great contributions in the fields of cardiac surgery and conservation. Charles A. Lindbergh died in 1974.

Games and toys celebrate aviation

Games and toys were popular ways for children to participate in the glory of American aviation advances. Included in this sample collection is the *Spirit of St. Louis* toy construction set.

The Ryan-built plane the *Spirit of St. Louis* was donated to the Smithsonian Institution in Washington, D.C., in 1928. Today, visitors to the National Air and Space Museum can see the actual plane Lindbergh flew across the Atlantic. What amazes everyone who sees it is how small it appears. It is 27 feet 8 inches in length and 9 feet 10 inches in height with a wingspan of 46 feet. Compare

Americans sang about Lindbergh

Following Lindbergh's daring flight, dozens of songs and poems were written to celebrate his feat.

that with a modern Boeing 737-200 passenger jet, which has a length of 100 feet, a height of 37 feet, and a wingspan of 93 feet.

Richard E. Byrd led several important explorations of Antarctica and was promoted to the rank of admiral. A proud graduate of the United States Naval Academy in Annapolis, Maryland, his name is engraved on an impressive tablet, located in the academy's Bancroft Hall, honoring graduates who were awarded the Congressional Medal of Honor, the highest award that a member of the United States Armed Services can receive. Byrd died in 1957.

After the *Columbia* flight, Clarence Chamberlin designed his own line of monoplanes and formed his own small airline, which proved unsuccessful. He tried his hand at several aviation endeavors, including flying schools, and ultimately worked in the real estate business in Connecticut. He died in 1976.

Charles A. Levine outlived them all. He died in 1991 at the age of ninety-four. After his historic flight, he found himself enmeshed in shady business dealings. When the Depression began in 1929, he lost most of his fortune. He was arrested by Vienna, Austria, police on a charge of counterfeiting gold coins. No sooner had that charge been dropped when he was accused by New York authorities of stealing stock certificates. Grace Levine's patience ended as did their marriage, with divorce in 1935. "First I do, then I think," Levine once said. In 1937, Levine was convicted on a federal charge of smuggling tungsten, a regulated material, from Canada for one of his businesses. He served a two-year prison sentence. In 1942, he was convicted in federal court of smuggling a German citizen into the country during wartime. The fact that the man was a Jewish escapee from a German concentration camp did not matter to the court. Levine was sentenced to serve 150 days in jail.

Pilot Wilbur Stultz made the first nonstop flight in the *Columbia* from New York to Havana, Cuba, in 1928. Two years later, the *Columbia* flew over the Atlantic once more after Levine and Chamberlin's historic flight. Renamed the *Maple Leaf*, the plane was destroyed in a hangar fire at the Bellanca factory in Newcastle, Delaware, on January 25, 1934.

The three successful transatlantic flights of 1927 secured aviation's future.

They demonstrated that airplanes could carry passengers and cargo between continents. Levine remarked, "I am the first American air tourist abroad. Seeing Europe by air is the only way for me." These flights also proved that, with proper preparations and better equipment, aviation could be relatively safe. The flights also changed the negative image of American pilots, who were generally viewed as unkempt daredevils. The world had become smaller overnight. No longer would any city on earth be isolated from another.

Each of the flights had a different impact. Lindbergh achieved near god-like fame not only because he was first, but he was also the perfect hero. He was young, photogenic, daring, pure in mind and body—a true symbol of the imagined American ideal. His lone flight into the unknown captivated the imagination of young and old alike. A movie, based on his Pulitzer Prize–winning book, starred Jimmy Stewart as Lindbergh. It gave millions of people a realistic glimpse of what it was like to fly the Atlantic alone. By flying the *Spirit* into each of the then forty-eight states, Canada, and Mexico, Lindbergh, the goodwill ambassador, did more to further the cause of aviation than any other person of his time.

The flight of Chamberlin and Levine in the *Columbia* established a world distance record. It demonstrated that Lindbergh's flight was not a fluke. Levine also had the distinction of being the first transatlantic passenger, signaling the future of passenger transportation. In the 1920s, Jews faced discrimination in American society. Jewish popular heroes were few. Charles A. Levine lifted the spirits of other Jewish Americans and briefly served as a positive role model because of his daring trip. Accounts of his trip appeared prominently in Jewish newspapers. A famous vaudeville song in Yiddish and English, "Levine and His Flying Machine," celebrated his daring flight. The *Buffalo Jewish News* offered the following opinions:

"It is not necessary for us to point out the intrepidity of a Levine to prove that the Jewish people are capable of acts of great courage. No nation has a monopoly on heroism."

"The memorable flight is also a remarkable event in the history of American

Jewry ... No other Jew in modern times has accomplished a feat as brave and worthy."

In a stage act in the 1927 *Ziegfeld Follies* on Broadway, comedian Eddie Cantor was asked to name all the famous aviators of 1927. Taking pride in the accomplishments of the Jewish flier, Cantor replied, "Well—Chamberlin, Levine, Ruth Elder, Levine, Commander Byrd, Levine." "Who else?" an actor asked. "Did I mention Levine?" Cantor replied.

Commander Richard E. Byrd and his crew emphasized the possibility of transatlantic passenger service. They proved that "a large, well equipped plane could span the Atlantic under adverse weather conditions even with relatively crude navigational equipment." Although the *America* met with disaster, the meticulous planning served as a model for how future flights should be organized.

When the hoopla of ticker-tape parades and adulation faded away, what remained was a growing public interest and confidence in aviation. The great air race of 1927 was over; its results are still felt today.

AUTHOR'S NOTE

My father was just a boy, but he remembered the event all his life—the day he saw Lindbergh. On Saturday morning, July 23, 1927, my father and his friends walked the five miles to Boston's Logan Airport to watch the pilot-hero take off in the *Spirit of St. Louis* for Concord, New Hampshire. Boston was only one of many stops for Lindbergh that year. Before this tour was over, Lindy visited each of the forty-eight states, Canada, and Mexico as aviation's goodwill ambassador.

Because the transatlantic flights of 1927 were so much in the news that year, newspapers of the era are wonderful resources for any researcher. The *New York Times* and local newspapers are available online as well as on microfilm in many public libraries.

Lindbergh, Chamberlin, and Byrd wrote detailed accounts of their flights, and readers may find their autobiographies of interest. Again, the public library is a good source for these books since most are now out of print.

The Smithsonian National Air and Space Museum in Washington, D.C., displays the original *Spirit of St. Louis*. A replica may be seen by travelers who visit the Lindbergh Terminal at the Minneapolis–St. Paul International Airport in Minnesota. The Minnesota Historical Society in St. Paul and the Missouri Historical Society in St. Louis contain memorabilia relating to Charles Lindbergh's life. Papers concerning his transatlantic flight are housed at the Yale University Library in New Haven, Connecticut.

SOURCE NOTES

The source of each quotation in this book is found below. The citation indicates the first words of the quotation and its document source. The sources are listed in the bibliography.

CHAPTER 1: The Shortest Distance   page 7

"I am attempting the flight …": Ault, p. 135.
"My own active interest …": Morris, p. 23.
"This flight lasted only …": Morris, p. 7.
"I should never ask …": Morris, p. 168.
"not to get too high …": Morris, p. 10.
"Newfoundland is a hospitable place …": Jablonski, p. 38.
"I followed the direction …": Jablonski, p. 48.
"We have had a terrible journey …": Jablonski, p. 49.
"The modern radial air-cooled …": Jablonski, p. 99.
"added to our chances …": Byrd, p. 168.

CHAPTER 2: Next Stop, Europe   page 20

"This is the moment …": Lindbergh, *Spirit*, p. 182.
"My ideas of airplane design…": Associated Press, 1927.
"thought it would be …": Columbia University Oral History Aviation Project, p. 3.
"I wonder why those …": Chamberlin, p. 30.
"To hell with the plane …: *Times of London*, p. 1.
"I told the girls …": Chamberlin, p. 31.
"Thank you for the ride …": Chamberlin, p. 33.
"You can sign it …": Chamberlin, p. 37.
"a flying gas tank …": Expressed frequently in several sources.
"Fuel comes first …": de La Croix, p. 63.
"Let's go …": *New York Times*, May 8, 1927.
"Nungesser off on …": *New York Times*, May 8, 1927.
"Luck has always been …": Montague, p. 57.
"I am glad and proud …": Montague, p. 56.
"Let's put everything …": Lindbergh, *Spirit*, p. 88.
"Three transatlantic planes …": *New York Times*, May 13, 1927.
"It's more like a funeral …": Lindbergh, *Spirit*, p. 178.
"A take-off seems …": Lindbergh, *Spirit*, p. 185.

CHAPTER 3: Lucky Lindy   page 37

"All I want …": Lindbergh, *Spirit*, p. 354.
"does not wish …": *New York Times*, March 3, 1927.
"Multiengined planes are more …": Lindbergh, *Spirit*, p. 59.
"a plane that's got …": Lindbergh, *Spirit*, p. 17.
"can complete in two months …": Wagner, p. 116.
"So you want to buy …": Lindbergh, *Spirit*, p. 72.
"We would contribute to …": Lindbergh, *Spirit*, p. 73.
"We will sell our plane …": Lindbergh, *Spirit*, p. 75.
"Recommend closing deal …": Lindbergh, *Spirit*, p. 85.
"They're as anxious to …": Wagner, p. 122.
"Why does this damn …": Wagner, p. 125.
"a flying gas tank …": Expressed frequently in several sources.
"Are you sure one …": Lindbergh, *Spirit*, p. 83.
"for the first time …": Wagner, p. 127.
"Supposing one of the others …": de La Croix, p. 87.
"Each moment I feel more …": Lindbergh, *Spirit*, p. 151.
"To hell with the money …": Lindbergh, *Spirit*, p. 169.
"We carried nothing but …": Lindbergh, *Spirit*, p. 5.
"If Lindbergh makes it …": Hamlen, p. 131.

SOURCE NOTES

"Due to Bellanca's resignation …": Hamlen, p. 132.
"living partner in adventure …": Lindbergh, *Spirit*, p. 210.
"little box with fabric walls …": Lindbergh, *Spirit*, p. 191.
"[M]y plane and my life …": Lindbergh, *Spirit*, p. 228.
"Each dial and lever …": Lindbergh, *Spirit*, p. 191.
"I don't plan on going …": Lindbergh, *Spirit*, p. 89.
"Windows would cut down …": Lindbergh, *Spirit*, p. 210.
"Up to the time I …": Lindbergh, *We*, p. 22.
"There's something in its rhythm …": Lindbergh, *Spirit*, p. 301.
"able to vanish or appear …": Lindbergh, *Spirit*, p. 389.
"I'll continue on my course …": Lindbergh, *Spirit*, p. 351.
"Which way is Ireland …": Lindbergh, *We*, p. 222.
"I stare at it intently …": Lindbergh, *Spirit*, p. 462.
"For nearly half an hour …": Lindbergh, *We*, p. 225.

CHAPTER 4: "Well, Here We Are." page 52
"Well, here we are …": *Time*, May 30, 1927, p. 14.
"I am very happy …": *Time*, May 30, 1927, p. 14.
"Oh, you don't have to …": *New York Herald Tribune, International Edition*, May 22, 1927, p. 1.
"You are a very brave …": *New York Times*, May 23, 1927, p. 1.
"demonstate[d] the reliability …": *New York Times*, May 25, 1927, p. 2.
"bring our peoples nearer …": Lindbergh, *We*, p. 244.
"I shall always regard …": *New York Times*, May 26, 1927, p. 1.
"Ah, but you, my son …": *New York Times*, May 26, 1927, p. 1.
"worse than I had …": *New York Times*, May 30, 1927, p. 1.
"What are you going to do …": Lindbergh, *We*, p. 256–7.
"Captain Lindbergh will now …": Lindbergh, *We*, p. 257.
"I bring a message home to you …": *New York Times*, June 12, 1927, p. 2.
"I don't give it to you …": *New York Times*, June 14, 1927, p. 1.
"Lindbergh uses Gargoyle Mobiloil …": Newspaper sources.
"a super hero who has …": *New York Times*, May 22, 1927, p. 1.
"The plane will be placed …": *New York Times*, May 22, 1927, p. 1.

CHAPTER 5: "To Berlin! To Berlin!" page 66
"We had plenty …": Charles A. Levine. *New York Times*, June 7, 1927, p. 1.
"Oh-h-h! He's not going? …": Ault, p. 156.
"What are you up to …": de La Croix, p. 102.
"it would be too far …": Jablonski, p. 141.
"I'd rather be in Davy Jones' …": Jablonski, p. 141.
"sat up one night …": Newspaper/archival files.
"Well, Admiral, I used Balchen's …": Columbia University Oral History Aviation Project, p. 5.
"This part of the …": Newspaper/archival files.
"Europe next stop …": Montague, p. 90.
"I was not at all sure …": Chamberlin, p. 57.
"She'll give a report …": Hamlen, p. 142.
"You want to know …": Columbia University Oral History Aviation Project, p. 7.
"I didn't know how to …": Columbia University Oral History Aviation Project, p. 7.
"You get so accustomed to …": *New York Times*, June 13, 1927, p. 4.
"My daughter, Eloyse, is going …": *New York Times*, June 13, 1927, p. 4.
"We'll have to get out …": Hamlen, p. 142.
"She appeared to have …": Chamberlin, p. 78.
"I want to go where …": Columbia University Oral History Aviation Project, p. 7.

SOURCE NOTES

"Where are you …": Chamberlin, p. 8.
"fly farther than anyone …": Chamberlin, p. 85.
"Following your flight …": Hamlen, p. 147.
"Charlie's is a greater …": Hamlen, p. 147.
"How I wish I'd been …": Hamlen, p. 147.
"Levine wanted me to fly …": Jablonski, p. 142.
"naturally disappointed that …": *New York Times*, June 6, 1927, p. 1.
"There was nothing more …": *New York Times*, June 12, 1927, p. 4.
"See what you can do with …": Jablonski, p. 143.
"bucking bronco …": Jablonski, p. 143.
"They're blast furnaces …": Chamberlin, p. 93.
"*Nach Berlin?* …": Chamberlin, p. 94.
"You're the doctor …": Jablonski, p. 144.

CHAPTER 6: "Far Enough!" page 74
"We have come …": Charles A. Levine. Newspaper/archival files.
"We didn't see how …": Chamberlin, p. 104.
"Are you all right …": Chamberlin, p. 106.
"Their sleep is sound …": *New York Times*, June 7, 1927, p. 1.
"The American people are …": *New York Times*, June 8, 1927, p. 1.
"When over here …": *New York Times*, June 12, 1927, p. 18.
"Will you fly back? …": Hamlen, p. 154.
"*Eins, zwei, [drei], Chamberlin* …": *New York Times*, June 11, 1927, p. 4.
"Of course I'll forgive …": Hamlen, p. 152.
"Levine's ways were …": *New York Times*, June 7, 1927, p. 1.
"You bet. I think …": *New York Times*, June 18, 1927, p. 1.
"meant to have …": *New York Times*, June 18, 1927, p. 1.
"She's some trick …": *New York Times*, June 18, 1927, p. 1.

CHAPTER 7: Close Enough page 88
"Can you visualize …": *New York Times*, July 20, 1927, p. 4.
"We wanted to show that …": Byrd, p. 227.
"personally went over every …": Byrd, p. 231.
"to demonstrate that passengers …": Byrd, p. 227.
"If anything went wrong …": Byrd, p. 226.
"If I were on my own …": Montague, p. 119.
"the most interminable …": Montague, p. 117.
"I admit it would …": Byrd, p. 232.
"Well, she's ready …": Hamlen, p. 166.
"empty our fuel in a …": Byrd, p. 228.
"putty-like substance …": Byrd, p. 261.
"When I reached the …": Byrd, p. 245.
"They're as good as …": Hamlen, p. 169.
"Whatta helluva take-off …": Hamlen, p. 171.
"Everything going fine …": Byrd, p. 171–2.
"Dense fog covers all …": Hamlen, p. 173.
"I hope no other …": Byrd, p. 255.
"This instrument flying is …": Montague, p. 124.
"If I were wrong …": Byrd, p. 257.
"We have seen neither …": Byrd, p. 260.
"It is impossible to …": Byrd, p. 258.
"It was a weird sight …": Byrd, p. 259.
"I made a mistake …": Byrd, p. 263.
"Hope to sight land …": Hamlen, p. 176.

SOURCE NOTES

"I am flying around …": Hamlen, p. 177.
"That makes three who …": *New York Times*, July 1, 1927, p. 4.
"They will never be …": *New York Times*, July 1, 1927, p. 2.
"Lost. Only three hours …": Hamlen, p. 177.
"They're there …": Montague, p. 129.
"Lost in the wind …": Hamlen, p. 177.
"I knew there was no …": Byrd, p. 267.
"There was nothing …": Byrd, p. 269.
"Stand by to land …": Byrd, p. 270.
"I am glad things …": *New York Times*, July 5, 1927, p. 1.
"Dick, where are you …": Hamlen, p. 180.
"We were stiff and …": Byrd, p. 275.
"Deeply sorry we did not …": *New York Herald*, July 2, 1927, p. 1.
"We are all overwhelmed …": *New York Herald*, July 2, 1927, p. 1.
"So long as we live …": Byrd, p. 277.

CHAPTER 8: Glory! page 101
"Levine's ways were …": *New York Times*, June 7, 1927, p. 1.
"That's too bad …": Hamlen, p. 181.
"Well done, Byrd! …": Hamlen, p. 181.
"I knew only too well …": Jablonski, p. 153.
"Apparently, Mr. Levine has …": Jablonski, p. 154.
"I really didn't appreciate …": Chamberlin, p. 162.
"with real sincerity and …": Chamberlin, p. 167.
"I had my day …": *New York Times*, July 19, 1927, p. 1.
"Good to be back …": *New York Times*, July 19, 1927, p. 1.
"The windows are jammed …": *New York Times*, July 19, 1927, p. 1.
"This seems to be my …": *New York Times*, July 19, 1927, p. 1.
"I think you are …": *New York Times*, July 19, 1927, p. 1.
"Can you visualize not …": *New York Times*, July 20, 1927, p. 4.
"We had a little more …": *New York Times*, July 20, 1927, p. 4.
"a flying man who …": Collinson, p. 131.
"I didn't see the ambulance …": *New York World*, October 18, 1927, p. 2.
"The arrival and subsequent …": Ault, p. 162.
"Hello, I think I need …": *New York Times*, August 30, 1927, p. 2.
"I'm fed up with the …": de La Croix, p. 122.
"I am no madcap …": *New York Times*, September 12, 1927, p. 1.
"the greatest man in …": *New York World*, October 18, 1927, p. 2.
"profound admiration …": *Jewish Advocate*, October 20, 1927, p. 5.
"He is a hero in my …": *New York World*, October 18, 1927, p. 2.
"You came back too …": *New York World*, October 18, 1927, p. 1.
"how proud we are …": *Jewish Advocate*, October 20, 1927, p. 1.
"The American people and the …": *New York World*, October 18, 1927, p. 1.
"Fate has been very …": *Jewish Advocate*, October 20, 1927, p. 1.

CHAPTER 9: Frontier of Flight page 114
"New York to Paris …": Lindbergh, *Spirit*, p. 14.
"Forty-two invaluable …": Hamlen, p. 182.
"Never heard a motor sound …": Montague, p. 84.
"First I do …": Newspaper/archival files.
"I am the first American air …": *New York Times*, July 1, 1927, p. 4.
"It is not necessary …": *Buffalo Jewish News*.
"The memorable flight …": *Buffalo Jewish News*.
"Well—Chamberlin, Levine …": Cantor, p. 189.
"a large, well equipped …": Morris, p. 266.

BIBLIOGRAPHY

BOOKS

Ault, Phil. *By the Seat of Their Pants: The Story of Early Aviation*. New York: Dodd, Mead, 1978.

Byrd, Richard E. *Skyward: Man's Mastery of the Air as Shown by the Brilliant Flights of America's Leading Air Explorer*. New York: G. P. Putnam's Sons, 1928.

Cantor, Eddie. *My Life Is in Your Hands*. New York: Blue Ribbon Books, 1932.

Chamberlin, Clarence D. *Record Flights*. Philadelphia: Dorrance, 1928.

Collinson, Clifford, and Captain F. McDermott. *Through Atlantic Clouds: The History of Atlantic Flight*. London: Hutchinson, 1934.

Dade, George C., and Frank Strnad. *Picture History of Aviation on Long Island, 1908–1938*. New York: Dover, 1989.

Gill, Brendan. *Lindbergh Alone*. New York: Harcourt Brace Jovanovich, 1977.

Hamlen, Joseph R. *Flight Fever*. Garden City, NY: Doubleday, 1971.

Hoare, Robert J. *Wings over the Atlantic*. Boston: C. T. Branford, 1957.

Jablonski, Edward. *Atlantic Fever*. New York: Macmillan, 1972.

La Croix, Robert de. *They Flew the Atlantic*. Translated by Edward Fitzgerald. New York: Norton, 1959.

Lindbergh, Charles A. *The Spirit of St. Louis*. New York: Scribner, 1953.

———. *We*. New York: G. P. Putnam's Sons, 1927.

Miller, Francis Trevelyan. *Lindbergh: His Story in Pictures*. New York: G. P. Putnam's Sons, 1929.

Montague, Richard. *Oceans, Poles, and Airmen: The First Flights over Wide Waters and Desolate Ice*. New York: Random House, 1971.

Morris, Lloyd, and Kendall Smith. *Ceiling Unlimited: The Story of American Aviation from Kitty Hawk to Supersonics*. New York: Macmillan, 1953.

The Reminiscenses of Clarence Chamberlin, Columbia University Oral History Aviation Project, 1960.

Spenser, Jay P. *Bellanca C.F.: The Emergence of the Cabin Monoplane in the United States*. Washington, DC: Smithsonian Institution Press, 1982.

Tessendorf, K. C. *Wings around the World: The American World Flight of 1924*. New York: Atheneum, 1991.

Wagner, William. *Ryan, the Aviator: Being the Adventures and Ventures of Pioneer Airman and Businessman, T. Claude Ryan*. New York: McGraw-Hill, 1971.

The following periodicals are cited in the Source Notes:

Buffalo (NY) *Jewish News*

Jewish Advocate (Boston)

New York Herald Tribune

New York Times

New York World

BIBLIOGRAPHY

WEB SITES*

www.nasm.si.edu
Smithsonian National Air and Space Museum
An authoritative source for the history of flight. Includes many photographs.

www.centennialofflight.gov
U.S. Centennial of Flight Commission
An informative site that focuses on early aviation, particularly in the United States.

www.century-of-flight.net
Century of Flight
Offers detailed information about the history of flight.

www.charleslindbergh.com
Charles Lindbergh, An American Aviator
Includes comprehensive details on all aspects of Lindbergh's life.

www.nsf.gov/news/special_reports/byrd/revisited.jsp
National Science Foundation
Although the site focuses on Richard Byrd's polar and Antarctic expeditions,
there are also references to his 1927 flight to France.

www.yiddishradioproject.org/exhibits/levine/levine.php3?pg=3
Yiddish Radio Project
A detailed and colorful look at the life of Charles A. Levine.

www.acepilots.com/pioneer/fokker_trimotor.html
Acepilots.com
Dedicated to the Fokker aircraft, including Richard Byrd's *America*.

www.history.nasa.gov/timeline.html
NASA History Division
A detailed timeline of aviation events from 1915 on.

*Active at the time of publication

INDEX

Page numbers in **boldface** refer to photographs.

A

Acosta, Bert, 25, 26, 43, 93, 94, 95, 98, 100, 106, 114
Aero Club (New York), 18
Albert (king of Belgium), 58
Alcock, John, 11
America (airplane), 21, 24, 26, **33**, 34, 36, 43, 44, 64, 65, 67, **68**, 88, **88**, 89, 90, **90**, 94, **94**, 114
  crash landing, 26, **99**, **101**
  June 29, 1927, flight, 87, 90–100
American Legion (airplane), 21, 28, 44
Atlantic (biplane), 11
Aviation and Aircraft (magazine), 38

B

Balchen, Bernt, 68, 69, 93, 94, 95, 98–100, 106, 108, 114
balloonists, 8
Bellanca, Giuseppe, 22, **23**, 25, 27, 32, 38, 39, 45, 65, 72
Bennett, Floyd, 17, 26
Berlin (ship), 84, 85
Bertaud, Lloyd, 26, 28, 32, 34, 65
Betsy Ross flag, 99, 102
Blériot, Louis, 8, 55, **56**
British Air Council, 58
Brooklyn Chamber of Commerce, 26, 27, 34, 71, 85
Brown, Arthur Whitten, 11, 12
Byrd, Richard E., 17, 21, 26, 29, 34, **35**, 37, 43, 45, 64, 65, 68, 72, 87, 88–103, 104, 105, 106, 114, 119
  Antarctic exploration, **89**
  Arctic exploration, **89**, 90
  Distinguished Flying Cross, 108
  reception in France, 102, 103, **103**
  reception in New York, 105, **105**, 106, **107**, 108

C

Cantor, Eddie, 121
Carisi, John, 27, 66, 68, 116

Chamberlin

Chamberlin, Clarence, 10, 24, 25, 26–28, 31, **35**, 43, 65–81, **78**, **81**, **83**, 84, 85, 86, **86**, **87**, 91, 92, 97, 102, **102**, 103, **103**, 104–106, **107**, 109, 113, 114, 119, 120
Churchill, Winston, 12
Clavier, Charles, 18, 19, 114
Coli, François, 29, **30**, 31, **31**, 32, 44, 57, 95, 114
Collier Trophy, 114
Columbia (airplane), 22, **23**, 28, 29, 31, 33, 34, 36, 37, 44, 45, **67**, **79**, **81**, 84, 90, 92, 93, 104, 112, **112**, 113, 114, 116, 119
  design, 32
  flight to Berlin (June 4, 1927), **76**, **77**, 78, **80**
  further flights, 85, 97, 104, 109–110, 119
  test flight (April 24, 1927), 26–28, 44
Coolidge, Calvin, 16, 18, 58, **60**, 61, 103
Cottbus (Germany), 75–79
Croydon Airfield (London), 71, 110
Curtin, Lawrence, 18
Curtiss Company, 10
Curtiss Field, 18, 20, 21, 26, 28, 32, 33, 34, 44, 64, 65

D

Daedalus, 7
Davis, Noel, 21, 28, 43, 44, 114
Douglas Aircraft Company
  biplanes, 15
  Boston (biplane), 15, 16
  Chicago (biplane), 15, 16
  New Orleans (biplane), 15, 16
  Seattle (biplane), 15, 16
Doumergue, Gaston, 55, **55**, 102
Drouhin, Maurice, 104, 109, 111
Dutch Flats Airfield, **24**, **25**

E

Edward, Prince of Wales (Great Britain), 58
Eisleben, 73

F

Fish, Hamilton, 113

INDEX

Fokker, Anthony, 9, 26, 91
Fokker airplane, 17, 89–90, **94**
Fonck, René-Paul, 9, **9**, 18–19, **19**

G
George V (king of England), 12, 58
Goldsborough, Brice, 116

H
Hall, Donald, 115
Hawker, Harry, 11
Hazelhurst Field, 20
Hempstead Plains Aerodrome, 20
Herrick, Myron T., 53, **55**, **57**
Hinchliffe, Walter, 111, **111**
Hindenburg, Paul von, 80

I
Icarus, 7
Islamoff, Jacob, 18, 19, 114

J
Jonas, Grace, 27
Jonas, Ralph, 85

K
Kimball, James H., 29, 32, 34, 69, 92–93, 114–115
Kinkaid, Harold, 93, 116

L
Lawrance, Charles L., 114
Le Bourget Airfield (Paris), 31, 50, 52, 55, **86**,
    96–98, **102**, 110
Le Matin (newspaper), **31**
Leonardo da Vinci, 8
Leviathan (ship), 104, 105, 113
Levine, Charles A., 22, 23, 24, 25, 26, 28, 32, 34,
    37, 39, 45, 65, 91, 97, 102, **102**, 103, 104, 109,
    112, 114, 116, 119
  Columbia Aircraft Corporation, 22
  flight to Germany, 66–85, **76**, **77**, **78**, **79**, **80**,
    81, **82**, **83**
  flight to London, 110, **111**, **112**

Jewish American, 77, 84, 120–121
  receptions in Europe, 84–86, **86**, **87**, 112
  return to New York, 113
Levine, Eloyse (daughter), 27, 28, 44, 69
Levine, Grace (wife), 26, 27, 66, 70, 84, 85, 109,
    110, 111, 113, 119
Levine, Isaac (father), 71
"Levine and His Flying Machine" (song), 120
Lilienthal, Otto, 7
Lindbergh, Anne Morrow (wife), **115**, 116
Lindbergh, Charles A., **19**, 21, 23, 33, 34, **35**, 36,
    38–39, 41–44, 57–59, **59**, 101, 102, 106, 114,
    115, 116, 123
  arrival and reception in Paris, 52–57, **53**, **54**,
    55, **56**, **57**
  childhood, **13**, 14, **14**
  Distinguished Flying Cross, 61
  early flying experiences, 10, 13, 14–15, **15**, 17,
    38, 44
  flight to Paris, 45–51
  meeting with Charles A. Levine, 39
  meeting with King George V, 58
  post-transatlantic flights, 58, 63–64, 120
  reception in New York, **62**, 63
  reception in Washington, **60**, 61, **61**
  song about, 64, **118**
Lindbergh, Charles A., Jr. (son), 116
London Daily Mail prize, 8, 11, 12
London Times, 110
Lufthansa, 78, 85

M
Mackenzie-Grieve, Kenneth, 11
Macom (ship), **62**, 63, 105, 106, 113
Mauretania (ship), 70, 71
McNamee, Graham, 106
Memphis (U.S. Navy ship), 58, 59
Missouri Historical Society, 64
Mitchel Field, 20, 27, 63
Mobil Oil Company, 64
Mussolini, Benito, 112

INDEX

N

National Air and Space Museum, 117
National Geographic Society, 18
Newfoundland, 8, 10, 11, 12, 46, 69, 95
New York Times, 21, 31, 33, 37, 57, 59, 69, 70, 71, 72, 76, 101
Noville, George, 93–96, 98, 99, 100, 106, 108, 114
Nungesser, Charles, 9, 29, **30**, 31, **31**, 32, 44, 57, 95, 114
Nungesser, Madame (mother), 32, 54, 103

O

Orteig, Raymond, 17
   Orteig Prize, **9**, 17, 18, 19, 21, 26, 32, 37, 38, 44, 63

P

Pioneer Instrument Company, 28, 116
Pius XI (pope), 112

R

Rasche, Thea, 85
Richthofen, Manfred von, 9, 84
Rickenbacker, Edward V., 9
Robertson Aircraft Corporation, 13, 38
Roosevelt Field, 18, **19**, 20, 21, 25, 26, 27, 28, 29, **33**, 34, 35, 36, 37, 51, 64, 66, 67, **67**, **87**, 89, 90, 91, 93, 94
Ryan, T. Claude, 33, 38, 39, 46
Ryan Airlines, 21, **22**, 23, **25**, 29, 38, 39, **40**, 41, **42**, 43, 45, 46, 115, 117

S

Schurman, Jacob, 79
Seaplane Division Number 1, 10
Sikorsky, Igor, 18
Sikorsky airplane, 18, **19**, 38
Smith, Alfred E., 63
Spirit of St. Louis (airplane), 21, **22**, 24, 29, 33, **35**, 36, 38, **42**, **43**, 43–51, 58, 63, 64, 71, 90, 92, 114, 115, 116, 117

   design of, **24**, **25**, **40**, **41**, **47**, **48**, **49**, 115
   "flying gas tank," 29, 41
   games, **117**
   Paris landing, **52**, 52–53, 55
Spirit of St. Louis, The (book), 116
Stultz, Wilbur, 119

T

Tempelhof Airfield, 76, 79, 80, **81**

U

United States Naval Academy, 119
United States Post Office, 13, 45
   mail on the *America*, 99
United States Weather Bureau, 29, 92, 114

V

Ver-sur-Mer (France), 98, 100, **101**, 104
Vickers-Vimy biplane, 11

W

Wade, Leigh, 24
Walker, James J., 63, 108, 113
Wanamaker, Rodman, 37, 63, 89, 100
Waterman Pen Company, 64
We (book), 46, 64
White Bird (airplane), 29, **30**, 31, 32
Wilbur, Curtis, 108
Wilson, Woodrow, 10
Wooster, Stanton H., 21, 28, 43, 44, 114
Wright, Orville, 7
Wright, Wilbur, 7
Wright Aeronautical Corporation, 17, 22, 25, 34, 38, 44, 63, 93, 116
   J-4 Whirlwind engine, 17
   J-5 Whirlwind engine, 17, 22, 23, 34, 46, 49, 63, 73, 90, 93, 114, 116
Wright-Bellanca airplane, 22, 23, **23**, 24, 27, 38, 39

Z

Ziegfeld Follies, 121

TEXT CREDITS

Columbia University Oral History Research Office, New York City, from "The Reminiscences of Clarence Chamberlin," 1960: 24; 68; 69; 70.

Doubleday, a division of Bantam Doubleday Dell Publishing Group, from *Flight Fever* by Joseph R. Hamlen. Copyright © 1971: 45; 70; 71; 81; 91; 93; 94; 96; 97; 98; 101; 115.

Macmillan Company, from *Ceiling Unlimited* by Lloyd Morris and Kendall Smith. Copyright © 1953: 7; 9; 10.

McGraw-Hill, Inc., from *Ryan, the Aviator* by William Wagner. Copyright © 1971: 39; 41; 42.

Random House, Inc., from *Oceans, Poles, and Airmen* by Richard Montague. Copyright © 1971: 32; 91; 95; 97; 116.

Simon and Schuster, Inc., from *The Spirit of St. Louis* by Charles A. Lindbergh. Copyright © 1953 by Charles Scribner's Sons; copyright renewed © 1981 Anne Morrow Lindbergh: 33; 36; 38; 39; 44; 46; 49; 50.

PICTURE CREDITS